# REARING RIGHTEOUS
# YOUTH OF ZION

*Great News,
Good News,
Not-So-Good News*

# REARING RIGHTEOUS YOUTH OF ZION

*Great News,*
*Good News,*
*Not-So-Good News*

Brent L. Top, Ph.D.
Bruce A. Chadwick, Ph.D.

BOOKCRAFT
Salt Lake City, Utah

Library of Congress Catalog Card Number 98-72184
ISBN 1-57008-407-6

First Printing, 1998

Printed in the United States of America

*Bring up your children in light and truth as the Lord has commanded.*

*. . . I make you a solemn and sacred promise that if you will do this, the time will come when, looking upon those you have created, nurtured, and loved, you will see the fruits of your nurturing and get on your knees and thank the Lord for His blessing to you.*

—PRESIDENT GORDON B. HINCKLEY
OCTOBER 1993 GENERAL CONFERENCE

# Contents

Preface      *ix*

1    Introduction: How Youth Can Survive in a Sinful Society    *1*

2    How Are the "Saturday's Warriors" Doing?
Great News, Good News, and Not-So-Good News    *25*

3    The Power of Peers: For Good or Evil    *45*

4    Putting on the Armor of God:
The Power of Personal Spirituality    *67*

5    The Family Connection: Seedbed of Strength    *97*

6    Help from Beyond the Veil: The Power of the Covenant    *145*

Index    *159*

# Preface

Shortly after President Gordon B. Hinckley had been ordained and set apart as the fifteenth President of The Church of Jesus Christ of Latter-day Saints, he spoke to the press assembled in the Joseph Smith Memorial Building in Salt Lake City. "We are concerned with the quality of family life within so many homes," he declared in a prepared statement. "The home is the seedbed of all true virtue. If proper values are not learned in the home, they are not likely to be learned anywhere." In outlining the concerns of the Brethren and in articulating what would be the areas of primary focus for his administration, the newly ordained prophet and seer further taught:

> The family is the basic element of society. It is so important. Good homes produce good people. Good homes become the foundation for the strength of any nation. Good homes are certainly the rock-bottom need of our nation and every nation: homes in which there is a father who stands at the head of home in love and kindness and who assumes the basic responsibility to provide for his family. And a mother stands as the queen of that home, equally beside her husband, and they have children whom they love and cherish and nourish, and who love them in return. (Press conference, Salt Lake City, March 13, 1995; quoted in *Teachings of Gordon B. Hinckley* [Salt Lake City: Deseret Book Co., 1997], pp. 207–8.)

Perhaps never before in the history of the world has the family been under greater assault from the adversary and in greater need for prophetic counsel and divine direction than today. With this need in mind, the First Presidency and Quorum of the Twelve Apostles on September 23, 1995, issued to the world a solemn proclamation on the sacred role of families. "Parents have a sacred duty to rear their children in love and righteousness," declared the proclamation, "to provide for their physical and spiritual needs, to teach them to love and serve one another, to observe the commandments of God and to be law-abiding citizens wherever they live." This inspired proclamation, written by modern prophets, seers, and revelators, further stated:

> The family is ordained of God. Marriage between man and woman is essential to His eternal plan. Children are entitled to be born within the bonds of matrimony, and to be reared by a father and a mother who honor marital vows with complete fidelity. Happiness in family life is most likely achieved when founded upon the teachings of the Lord Jesus Christ. Successful marriages and families are established and maintained on principles of faith, prayer, repentance, forgiveness, respect, love, compassion, work and wholesome recreational activities. ("The Family—A Proclamation to the World," *Ensign,* Nov. 1995, p. 102.)

Over the last several years we have been studying how youth of the Church deal with the temptations that surround them. We have examined the pressures they face from their peers and the influence the gospel has on them. In addition, we have studied the effects the family has on these teens and how the family can and does counteract the negative influences of today's wicked world. This book reports on that study. But more than just a research report, this book contains insightful comments from hundreds of teenagers and young adults regarding their personal challenges, the role of religion in their lives, and what their parents did and do to fortify them from the "fiery darts of the wicked." One of the major purposes of this book is to illustrate with empirical evidence, as well as personal experiences of teens and families, how the teachings of the gospel and the inspired teachings of the prophets and apostles do indeed bless families and strengthen youth in these troubled times.

Some readers may feel bogged down with statistical results and scientific terminology, whereas others may want more empirical evidence and less commentary. We have tried to balance the two.

As we draw from all of these important sources—statistical analysis, anecdotal comments of the youth, statements from Church leaders, common sense, and personal experience—we begin to get a better perspective on the power of faith and family in the lives of teens today. In presenting the results of our study and offering practical suggestions gleaned from years of research and working with youth—and through our own personal challenges in rearing our own families—our desire is to extend help and hope to parents everywhere. We know how difficult it is to be a parent in today's world. We know somewhat concerning the challenges our youth face. We know how desperate many parents are to receive any help possible in rearing righteous children. We have seen into the eyes of heartbroken parents who are weary and worn down from trying to rescue their teens from evil influences. We know firsthand the worries that weigh on parents' minds today.

Our greatest hope is that this book will show that parental help can be found in the spiritual teachings of the gospel and the practical guidance and counsel we receive from latter-day prophets. In addition to help, we desire that this book will extend hope to parents and children—a hope that comes from the principles and covenants of the gospel and a hope in Christ. With this kind of help and hope guiding our efforts as parents, we can rest assured that we are not left alone to raise our families in a wilderness of sin. Thus, our desire is that this book will not only put information in your heads and inspiration in your hearts, but that the ideas contained herein will be translated into actual practice in your homes and in the personal lives of parents and teenagers alike.

As is almost always the case with any worthy project, we have benefited from the important research of others in the field. Our work builds on a foundation laid by other competent researchers at Brigham Young University. We express appreciation to those colleagues who have been most influential in establishing this legacy. Stan Albrecht, David Alcorn, Darwin Thomas, Boyd Rollins, Marie Cornwall, and Brian Barber have spent much of their careers investigating adolescent development and the formative power of religion and family. This work has also benefited from the feedback and help we have received from our other colleagues in Sociology, Religious Education, and the Center for the Studies of the Family at Brigham Young University. To them and others who have inspired and assisted in many ways, we express our thanks.

We wish to express appreciation to our secretaries, Norene Petersen of Sociology and Laura Card of Religious Education, for all their help on this project. A special thanks also to Janice Garrett, a graduate student in Sociology, who contributed considerably to this project with her research and data analysis skills. Most of all, we express our deep love and appreciation to our wives, Wendy Top and Carolyn Chadwick, and our families for their support, encouragement, and love. The most important lessons we have learned about rearing righteous families in today's sinful society have come from them.

# 1

# INTRODUCTION:

## HOW YOUTH CAN
## SURVIVE IN A SINFUL SOCIETY

*This know also, that in the last days perilous times shall come.*

*For men shall be lovers of their own selves, covetous, boasters, proud, blasphemers, disobedient to parents, unthankful, unholy,*

*Without natural affection, trucebreakers, false accusers, incontinent, fierce, despisers of those that are good,*

*Traitors, heady, highminded, lovers of pleasure more than lovers of God.*

*—2 Timothy 3:1–4*

## A Wicked World

The Apostle Paul's warnings to his young disciple Timothy concerning the wicked conditions of the last days are now being realized before our very eyes. In fact, it may be even worse than Paul's dire description. Today we see all manner of sin—violence, crime, alcohol, and drug abuse, and the many faces of immorality, including pornography, premarital sex, and teenage pregnancies—all around us. Frighteningly, such concerns seem to be escalating at an alarming pace. Just as the Savior prophesied concerning the conditions in the world that would precede his Second Coming, "iniquity [does] abound, the love of men [does] wax cold" (Joseph Smith—Matthew 1:30) and "all things [are] in commotion; and surely, men's hearts [do] fail them; for fear [has] come upon all people" (D&C 88:91). Members of the Church certainly find themselves in the midst of such world conditions. We are witnessing, as the scriptures attest, that Satan "maketh war with the saints of God, and encompasseth them round about" (D&C 76:29). "We of all men, should not be surprised to see wickedness increase—though we deplore it," President Ezra Taft Benson observed. "Nor should we be surprised to see a rising increase in divorces, family break ups, moral problems, infidelity, unchastity, and every conceivable evil. The Savior said that iniquity would abound, and because of it the love of many will wax cold in the latter days." (*The Teachings of Ezra Taft Benson* [Salt Lake City: Bookcraft, 1988], p. 409.)

Prophets and Church leaders have long warned of such an onslaught of evil. This all-out attack by Satan and his angels is aimed not only at the youth—the valiant "Saturday's warriors" who have been reserved to come forth in these last days—but also at the homes and families into which these faithful spirits come. So stated former Presiding Bishop Victor L. Brown:

At the present time, there are wars and rumors of wars. Yet, may I suggest that there is another war currently going on in the world—a war more destructive than any armed conflict—yes, a war between good and evil, between freedom and slavery, between the Savior and Satan. Satan's legions are many. In their battle to enslave mankind, they use weapons such as selfishness; dishonesty; corruption; sexual impurity, be it adultery, fornication, or homosexuality; pornography; permissiveness; drugs; and many others. I believe Satan's ultimate goal is to destroy the family, because if he would

2

destroy the family, he will not just have won the battle; he will have won the war. (*Ensign,* Jan. 1974, p. 108.)

President Ezra Taft Benson further underscored this with seeric clarity:

> We live today in a wicked world. Never in our memory have the forces of evil been arrayed in such a deadly formation. The devil is well organized and has many emissaries working for him. His satanic majesty has proclaimed his intention to destroy our young people, to weaken the home and family, and to defeat the purposes of the Lord Jesus Christ through His great Church. (*The Teachings of Ezra Taft Benson,* p. 413.)

> Never have the forces of evil been so insidious, widespread, and enticing. Everywhere there seems to be a cheapening, weakening, downgrading of all that is fine, good, and uplifting—all aimed at our youth, while many of their parents are lulled away into a false security as they enjoy their comfortable complacency. (*The Teachings of Ezra Taft Benson,* p. 409.)

It is not just religious leaders and families of faith that are frightened by the escalation of evils and ills in society, the many threats to our youth, and the breakdown of the family. In 1992, then—United States Attorney General William Barr raised this alarm about what is happening in today's society:

> The most significant feature of contemporary society has been the battering of the family and its disintegration. Today, in America, we have soaring illegitimacy rates. Today, almost 30 percent of children are born out of wedlock—about a quadrupling in 25 years. In many inner-city areas, the illegitimacy rate is as high as 80 percent. And America also now has among the highest divorce rates in the world—divorce is as common as marriage. As a consequence of

this, we now have the highest percentage of children living in single-parent households.

This breakdown of the family is particularly distressing because it is the family that is the primary institution by which we conduct moral education—by which we transmit moral values from generation to generation. As the family is weakened, so is our ability to transmit values to the next generation.

And, it is the breakdown of the family that is at the root of most of our social problems today. ("The Judeo-Christian Tradition vs. Secularism," address delivered at the Catholic League for Religious and Civil Rights, Washington, D.C., 6 Oct. 1992.)

Satan assaults our youth in a variety of disturbing ways. A national commission comprised of educational, political, medical, and business leaders concluded that today's youth are facing challenges and problems almost unheard of in previous generations. This commission found that "suicide is now the second leading cause of death among adolescents, increasing 300 percent since 1950." In addition:

Teen pregnancy has risen 621 percent since 1940. More than a million teenage girls get pregnant each year. Eighty-five percent of teenage boys who impregnate them eventually abandon them.

The teen homicide rate has increased 232 percent since 1950. Homicide is now the leading cause of death among fifteen- to nineteen-year-old minority youth.

Every year substance abuse claims younger victims with harder drugs. A third of high school seniors get drunk once a week. The average age for first-time drug use is now thirteen years old.

This disturbing report on America's youth, which also grabbed the attention of Congress, reached this shocking, yet revealing, conclusion:

4

The challenges to the health and well-being of America's youth are not primarily rooted in illness or economics. Unlike the past, the problem is not childhood disease or unsanitary slums. The most basic cause of suffering . . . is profoundly self-destructive behavior. Drinking. Drugs. Violence. Promiscuity. A crisis of behavior and belief. A crisis of character. (*Imprimis,* Sept. 1991, p. 1; quoted by Gordon B. Hinckley in *Ensign,* May 1992, pp. 69–70.)

Not only does this paint a frightening picture of delinquency in America today, but it also portends worse to come. Teenagers comprised 7 percent of the U.S. population in 1995, yet they committed 31 percent of all violent crimes, including murder, rape, robbery, and aggravated assault. In light of these statistics, Dr. James Alan Fox, dean of Criminal Justice at Northeastern University in Boston, declared concerning teen violence that "we are facing a bloodbath of violence in the years ahead that will make 1995 look like the good old days." These truly are troubled times.

## *Temptations Faced by Youth*

It is bad enough to read these statistics and learn of individual cases of youth gone bad in newspapers and magazines and on the television, but it becomes profoundly personal when we see gang violence, pervasive promiscuity, and drug abuse invading our own neighborhoods and surrounding our children in their schools.

The temptations that youth face today are potentially more dangerous than what earlier teens may have faced. Youth in the Church today seem to be more polarized than the teenagers of previous generations—they are either spiritually strong and dealing well with temptation or falling prey to the ways of the world at earlier and earlier ages. There seem to be fewer and fewer LDS teenagers occupying the middle ground. The number of exceptionally spiritual young people is humbling. But at the same time, more and more of the youth are not just temporarily "sowing wild oats" but actually are becoming lost souls whose lives are in nearly total disarray. These lost souls quickly wander so far off the strait and narrow path and become so involved in the evils of the day that they are damaged not only spiritually but ofttimes physically and emotionally—with long-term negative effects on their relationships with others and their educational and professional growth.

One reason for this polarization of the youth is that they feel enormous pressures tugging them in what is often two different directions—to live the gospel and at the same time to be accepted by their friends. They are struggling to live in the world, but not to be of the world. *"My parents really have no idea how hard it is to be a teenager today,"* one LDS high school student despaired. *"Almost all of my friends use alcohol and drugs and go to parties almost every weekend. Many are immoral and tell me how fun it is. When I tell them these things are against my religion, they make fun of me and call me names."* Another teen described the tension he felt between his desire to live the gospel and wanting to be accepted by his friends: *"I don't know what it is; I guess it is a desire to fit in or to be popular. I am a little shy, and sometimes when I'm around my friends I feel I have to make them like me, and then I do things I know are wrong. But if I don't do these things, I am rejected and feel isolated."* Days, weeks, and months of peer pressure can wear down the spiritual strength of youth and may cloud their view of right and wrong. Another LDS young woman eloquently described this process: *"From seeing my friends do things which were wrong, and not wanting to be made fun of, it is hard for me to fully understand what's right and wrong and sometimes I do things I regret later."*

## *The Challenge of Parenthood*

Parents are also facing greater pressures today than their parents and grandparents did in raising their families. There are greater demands on the time and resources of today's parents, which cause them to also feel tugged in many different directions. LDS parents often lie awake at night worrying about their children, wondering what they can do to help a son or daughter who is surrounded by, and may be yielding to, temptation. All parents want the best for their children and want them to be competent and successful in a demanding modern world. But for Latter-day Saint parents there is an additional expectation, with its accompanying pressure—to raise their children to be spiritually sound with testimonies of the gospel, their lives firmly founded on gospel principles and spiritually equipped to resist the temptations and powerful pressures they face daily. The question that haunts parents is, "How do we accomplish this?"

What can parents and youth leaders do to counteract the evil pressures that assault teenagers today? How can they help the youth of the Church "put on the armor of God?" What can be done to help youth gain their own testimonies and develop spiritual strength? What must occur within the family to insulate the youth from these evil influences? Is it better to raise children in the heart of Zion where there is a supportive LDS environment, or is it better to raise them in the mission field where they have to stand up for their beliefs? These are but a few of the many questions that parents ask themselves as they struggle to raise happy, competent, and faithful children in these trying times.

## The Study of LDS Youth

We designed a research project that was conducted through the Center for the Studies of the Family at Brigham Young University to provide some answers to the questions asked above. This research builds on a twenty-five-year legacy of research conducted at Brigham Young University by LDS scholars Dr. Darwin Thomas, Dr. Marie Cornwall, and Dr. Brian Barber. The results of this study, which we will discuss at length in this book, reveal how LDS youth are faring in the world today in comparison to their peers. We will also share insights into what factors are most influential in helping teenagers "put on the armor of God" that will help them to "withstand the evil day" and "quench all the fiery darts of the wicked" (see D&C 27:15–18).

## *The Power of Peers*

Almost every study of juvenile delinquency has discovered that peer pressure is the single most important factor leading to such behavior. Most parents do not need social research to tell them the influence that friends, or the lack thereof, have in the lives of teenagers. Most parents have witnessed a youth—their own child or someone else—who is surrounded by loyal friends who share his or her triumphs and who commiserate during times of disappointment. Most parents have also watched the devastation wrought when a young man or woman is ignored by other youth, or even worse when one is singled out for teasing, mocking, or bullying. As youth pass through adolescence it seems that being accepted by peers and having at least one close friend becomes of paramount importance. Perhaps this is because the family is too far removed from school, and youth need more immediate support in their daily struggles.

The high school students in the study were asked what was the strongest influence to live the principles of the gospel and then what was the strongest influence to not do so. Interestingly, peers or friends were mentioned most often in the answers to both questions. Youth told how good friends were a steady anchor to which their own righteousness was attached. *"My family and my friends have been the strongest pressures to live the standards of the Church,"* one young woman stated. She continued: *"I know I've been blessed with good friends that are members of the Church and that have helped me be a better person. I can see the effects bad friends have on people and I'm thankful for the ones I have."* Another young woman explained how she and her friends together live gospel-centered lives: *"I am blessed that I have great friends with the same high standards as me. For fun we, well, for example, we had a sleep-over at my house and we read the scriptures, shared personal experiences, and stuff like that. We have fun but also have the Spirit with us. And we're not what you might call nerds. We are friends with a lot of people at school."* It is interesting that this young woman is quick to point out that even though she and her friends try to live so as to have the Spirit in their lives, they still have fun and are not considered as dreaded "nerds."

Youth also reported that their friends, more than any other influence, were the cause of their failing to keep the commandments. Peer pressures, in the words of the young people, work in several ways. Obviously, sometimes friends or associates put direct pressure on a teenager to participate in a forbidden activity. Challenges to not be a "chicken," "wimp," or a similar unpopular thing are hard for adolescents to resist. Friends are also powerful role models regardless of whether they pressure. Watching friends drinking or doing drugs, seemingly having a good time, and at the same time being held in high esteem by classmates is an enticing example.

Friends' ideas can also influence a young person's sense of right or wrong. Several youth lamented how hard it was for them to know what was wrong when their friends packaged sin so attractively. Finally, the young, and to a degree all of us, desire to fit in, to be accepted in the group, to at least not draw unwanted attention to ourselves. The youth in many ways mentioned wanting to be accepted, to fit in, to be popular, to look good, to be cool and so on.

These pressures from friends are clearly articulated by a young woman who wrote: *"Public schools expose you to very awful, vulgar language and gestures. Bad people. I'm forced to see and hear bad things they do and say. A year ago I had some bad friends who pressured me to do bad things. At first it wasn't such obviously bad things. But when I'd lower my standards to their level, they'd lower theirs more."* A young man reported that *"the biggest negative pressure to not live the gospel is wanting to 'fit in' with everyone and doing wrong things just so I will fit in."* Another said, *"I want to be like everyone else and I want to be accepted in the group. The pressures get worse every year!"*

Thus, based on social research, our own experience as parents, and also our years of service as bishops, we included two types of peer pressures in our study of delinquency among LDS youth. We included both the obvious pressure to participate in delinquent activities and the pressure of example as measured by the proportion of friends who engage in delinquent behavior even though they do not pressure the LDS youth to join in the inappropriate activity.

## *The Shield of Faith*

We started with faith in the assumption that those youth who participate in the gospel plan less often fall prey to Satan's wiles. For generations, people assumed that training young people in religious values was a major factor in preventing crime, violence, and other unethical and immoral behaviors. In our day, however, this assumption has been rejected by most social scientists. Since they do not acknowledge such a thing as spiritual transformation, they resist any suggestion that religious values in and of themselves can be a valuable tool in combating societal ills. Studies conducted in the 1960s found that church attenders were "no more likely than non-attenders to accept ethical principles." Furthermore, they concluded that belonging to and attending a church was "unrelated to the commission of delinquent acts" (Travis Hirschi and Rodney Stark, "Hellfire and Delinquency," *Social Problems,* Fall 1969, p. 202). Numerous other studies later produced mixed results: some suggested that religious values deter delinquency, others found no such relationship. Some suggested that religion could discourage offenses against morals, such as drinking and premarital sex, but not legal offenses like robbing or assault.

To investigate the relationship between religious activity and delinquency among LDS youth, researchers from Brigham Young University conducted a study of high-school age LDS youth from various communities in Utah, southeastern Idaho, and southern California in the 1970s. They found that contrary to most of the social theory and research of the day, the more religious LDS teens were, the less involved they were in delinquent behaviors (Stan L. Albrecht, Bruce A. Chadwick, and David S. Alcorn, "Religiosity and Deviance: Application of an Attitude-Behavior Contingent-Consistency Model," *Journal for the Scientific Study of Religion,* Sep. 1977, pp. 263–74). Those LDS youth who not only believed in the gospel but also attended their meetings and prayed regularly reported significantly fewer delinquent actions than those who were not religiously inclined.

Some scholars reinterpreted the findings of this early study of LDS youth and argued that it was not the religious values the youth possessed that affected their behavior but rather the religious environment or "ecology" in which they lived. These social scientists argued that the active LDS youth in the study had lower levels of delinquency, such as dishonesty, vandalism, drug and alcohol use, and sexual immorality, because they lived in predominantly LDS communities and the social pressure to conform to LDS standards reduced their deviance (see Rodney Stark, "Religion and Conformity: Reaffirming a Sociology of Religion," *Sociological Analysis* [1984],

45:273–81; also "Religion as Context: Hellfire and Delinquency One More Time," *Sociology of Religion* [1996], 2:163–73). According to the religious ecology theory, an active young man's high school teacher may also be his bishop, or an active young woman's soccer coach may also be her Young Women adviser, and since virtually all of the youth's friends are also LDS, this pervasive religious culture pressures them to conform to Church standards. This theory rejects the idea that Latter-day Saint youth actually internalize religious principles that guide their behavior. This ecology theory predicts that an LDS youth living in a predominantly LDS community experiences greater social pressure to conform and thereby keeps gospel standards better than a youth living in an area where he or she is but one of a handful of LDS students in the high school. If the religious ecology theory held true for LDS youth, it would mean that LDS youth from communities in the "heart of Zion" would be significantly less involved in delinquent and immoral activities than LDS teenagers growing up elsewhere.

Based both on our experience as university professors and social science researchers and on our many years of experience as bishops, priesthood leaders, and advisers of youth—and as parents of teens ourselves—we were convinced that this ecology theory did not explain the behavior of LDS youth. Both of us have also lived with our families in areas outside of Utah where our children were often the only LDS kids in their schools. Having observed the youth in areas characterized as a low religious ecology, we were confident that other more important factors were leading the lives of young people away from delinquency than merely the religious-social culture in which they lived.

Many of the earlier studies that examined the relationship between religion and adolescent delinquency had focused mainly on religious affiliation—church membership—and whether the teen regularly attended any church. We recognized that to Latter-day Saints, being religious is much more than mere attendance at church meetings, or even professed beliefs. As a result, we examined five different aspects of religiosity. *Private religious behavior* involves personal prayer, scripture reading, fasting, and paying tithing. The frequency of attendance at various church meetings and functions is the substance of *public religious behavior.* The acceptance of traditional Christian beliefs and unique LDS doctrines constitutes *religious beliefs.* Another aspect of religious life is *spiritual experiences,* such as having prayers answered, having felt the Holy Ghost, and similar experiences. Finally, *acceptance in Church* measures how well youth felt they fit into their ward or branch and how accepted they felt by their fellow church members and leaders. These five dimensions of religiosity enabled us to ascertain whether religion does indeed deter delinquency among youth and which dimension, if any, is more effective than others in doing so.

## *Home and Family*

Although teenagers are seeking some form of independence from parents, the family remains an important source of emotional support and guidance during adolescence. A recent report about a national study of over 12,000 junior and senior high school students confirmed that the family continues to be a major source of support for American youth ("Protecting Adolescents from Harm: Findings from the National Longitudinal Study on Adolescent Health," Michael D. Resnick and associates, in *The Journal of the American Medical Association,* Sep. 10, 1997). These researchers noted that the main threats to teenagers' health are the risk behaviors in which they choose to engage: smoking, drinking, using drugs, participating in premarital sex, and engaging in violence obviously have serious consequences in the lives of youth. They further discovered in this research that the family, bonding between parent and youth, time parents spend with their teens, and parents' expectations for their children's school performance all made a difference in insulating youth from self-destructive behavior. They concluded, "With notable consistency across the domains of risk, the role of parents and family in shaping the health of adolescents is evident" (Resnick, p. 8).

Researchers have long puzzled over the effect divorce has on teenage children. Rather mixed results have emerged as studies of large samples of teens have not found much difference in school performance and delinquency between adolescents whose parents divorced and those raised in two-parent families. On the other hand, clinical studies of small numbers of teens who have been interviewed in-depth by a therapist have found significant emotional and social damage. The most widely known study has followed the children from sixty families in California who experienced a divorce (see *Second Chances: Men, Women and Children a Decade After Divorce*, Judith S. Wallerstein and Sandra Blakeslee [Boston: Hughton Mifflin Company, 1996]). The authors concluded that

> in the 1980s, people had the comforting illusion that divorce was a time-limited crisis, that children were resilient, and that within a year or two at the most everyone in the family would settle down and life would improve for all. . . . But that is not what our research revealed . . . [for] the men, women, and children whom we interviewed were still deeply affected by the divorce ten and fifteen years later. For them the breakup and its aftermath were life-shaping events. Their words bespoke a different experience, one that resonates into the 1990s. (Wallerstein and Blakeslee, 1996, p. xiii.)

Therefore we included family structure in this study—whether a two-parent or a single-parent family. Some researchers have studied whether it is family conflict or divorce itself that has an impact on teenagers. These studies have discovered that conflict in the home is not good for children and affects the school behavior and delinquency of teenagers. Thus, we also included the youth's perception of the conflict level between mother and father in the study.

Considerable research has also focused on how a mother's being employed outside the home affects a child's development. Unfortunately, little of this research has been directed at teenagers. Some believe that teens whose mothers work are not supervised as well as those whose moms are at home when the teens return from school. As bishops we occasionally dealt with cases where teens had skipped school and gone to a home from which mom was absent because of employment; here the youth did things that consequently required their bishop's attention. On the other hand, some argue that a working mother teaches teenagers responsibility and self-reliance as they have to assume greater accountability for household chores and their own care. To test these two arguments, we included maternal employment in our study to see if LDS teens whose mothers work participate in more delinquency than teens with a stay-home mom.

Based on recent research searching for an understanding of adolescent behavior, three important aspects of the relationship between parents and their teens were examined in this study—connectedness, regulation, and psychological autonomy. *Connectedness* is the teens' feelings that their father and mother love them and are genuinely interested in them. It includes the affection that exists between them and the emotional support they feel. Adolescents who have grown up feeling connected to their parents do better in school, get along better with others, and participate less in delinquency than those whose relationship with their parents was more distant.

*Regulation* involves rules, limit-setting, monitoring, and the discipline parents establish for their teenage children. Families who have guiding principles, a set of rules, a family constitution, or some other type of expectation provide their teenage children with guidelines about what is right and wrong and how to interact with other people in social settings. These family rules set bounds for teens to keep their behavior within when they are at school, at work, on dates, or hanging out with friends. When parents monitor their teens' behavior and hold them accountable by praising them for obedience and disciplining them for disobedience, they teach one of life's greatest lessons—that their behavior has very real consequences. Friends, teachers, neighbors, employers, store clerks, and even strangers expect them to behave in an appropriate manner, and infractions of social convention, good taste, or the law will result in consequences ranging from a frown or disapproving smirk to serious time in jail or prison. Parents who are overly lenient with their children don't do them a favor: they aren't showing greater love; rather they are leaving them to learn this important lesson from strangers who may be rather forceful in so doing. Teens who grow up with too little regulation become more heavily involved in deviant behavior. They have not learned self-control and are thus more likely to act impulsively and are more susceptible to negative peer influence, both of which lead to immoral or delinquent behavior.

*Psychological autonomy* refers to the degree to which teenagers are allowed to express their own thoughts, feelings, and opinions. Some parents control their children through interrupting them when they speak, rejecting their ideas or feelings as "stupid" or "unimportant," and threatening not to love them if they don't live up to the parents' precise expectations. Children who grow up with limited psychological autonomy lack confidence in their own ideas and opinions and have been found to experience depression and participate in more delinquency than youth granted greater autonomy. This is probably because their parents have interfered with the development of confidence in their own ideas and feelings. They therefore withdraw inside themselves or strike out against authority.

These parenting practices—connection, regulation, and autonomy—have proven useful in understanding the behaviors and prob-

16

lems of teenagers not only in the United States but also in several foreign countries. We anticipated that these practices would be equally relevant to understanding LDS teenagers as well.

## Study Objectives

We had two major objectives with this investigation. First, we tested the "religious ecology theory" to determine if the religious culture of the youth's community is more of an indicator of delinquent or immoral behaviors than is the degree to which the youth has made religious values an integral part of his or her own life. We collected information from LDS high school students in three geographic regions—the East Coast (from upstate New York to North Carolina), the Pacific Northwest (Seattle, Washington and Portland, Oregon areas), and Utah County in Utah (Lehi, American Fork, Orem, Provo, Springville areas). These three areas were chosen because they each represent a different religious "ecology." The Pacific Northwest has been identified by social scientists as having the lowest religious ecology in the United States. The East Coast is considered a moderate religious ecology, and the almost exclusively LDS communities of Utah County constitute the strongest religious ecology in the entire country. A religious ecology is generally ascertained by the proportion of the population that is affiliated with a religious denomination, the average frequency of church attendance, the number of church buildings, the number of clergy, the number of religious books sold or checked out of libraries, and other similar religious indicators per 100,000 population. Comparing the relationship between religiosity and delinquency in the three different religious ecologies provides evidence about whether LDS teens internalize religious principles that guide their behavior.

The second objective of the study was to determine the relationship between friends, family, religion, and delinquency by testing the model shown in figure 1. A model involves using several different influences—in this case peer pressures, religiosity, and family characteristics and processes—to explain delinquency. These factors work together to account for delinquency, and their combination is anticipated to be a much more powerful explanation than if we simply considered them one by one. In the real world, the influence of friends is combined with the influence of the family and church to impact the behavior of a teen. The model we tested considered all these influences together to understand why some youth are delinquent and others are not.

## Collecting Information

With the cooperation of the Church Educational System and the approval of the respective Area Presidents, three samples were drawn from the prospective seminary enrollment lists of LDS ninth through twelfth graders. Between 1992 and 1996 packets were sent to the parents of the approximately 4,000 LDS youth selected from the lists. A letter explained the objectives of the research and requested that they allow their teenage son or daughter to participate in the study. Parents were informed that the questionnaire asked about sensitive topics, including premarital sexual activity, drug use, and other delinquent behaviors. The letter to the parents stressed that in order to collect accurate information, they needed to allow their teen to respond in complete privacy. A letter to the youth and a business reply envelope was enclosed along with the questionnaire so that the teen could confidentially return the completed questionnaire. Postcard reminders and two follow-up mailings of new packets were sent to those who had not completed the questionnaire during a two-month period. These procedures resulted in a total of 3,103 respondents—1,393 from the East Coast, 632 from the Pacific Northwest, and 1,078 from Utah County. The smaller sample from the Pacific Northwest was selected because priesthood leaders requested it. Nearly 70 percent of the youth in the three samples responded by sending back a completed questionnaire. This is a reasonably high response rate for a mail survey, especially one involving teenagers and dealing with such sensitive issues.

## *Measurement*

The questionnaire asked these youths about their involvement in various delinquent behaviors, their exposure to peer pressures, religious beliefs and practices, and family characteristics and home environment. Forty questions asked whether the youth had *ever* participated in three different types of delinquency—offenses against others, offenses against property, and victimless offenses. *Offenses against others* involved such behaviors as bullying and fighting. *Offenses against property* involved things like shoplifting, vandalism, and stealing. Smoking, drinking, drug use, and various forms of immorality were categorized as *victimless or status offenses.*

To assess the extent of peer influence, we asked the teens in the study how many of their closest friends were also members of the Church, the extent to which they believed their friends were involved in the same forty delinquent behaviors (*peer example*), and to what degree their friends pressured them to participate in these illicit activities (*peer pressure*).

We asked several questions about each dimension of religiosity. Frequency of attendance at meetings and activities were used to indicate *public religious behavior.* How often the youth have personal prayer, read the scriptures by themselves, fast, and similar activities were indicators of *private religious behavior.* Acceptance of traditional Christian beliefs as well as unique LDS beliefs were measures of *religious beliefs.* The frequency of having felt the Spirit guide them or comfort them and how often their prayers had been answered were the indicators of *spiritual experiences*. Finally, feelings of belonging, of being welcome in the ward, and of acceptance in Young Men or Young Women's programs were used to assess *acceptance in Church.*

Several questions about the feelings between the youth and their parents were used to indicate the degree of *connectedness*. Previous research has discovered that the broad range of *regulating* parenting activities can be accurately gauged by questions about how closely the youth feel their parents monitor their behavior. We used these questions to measure *regulation*. Earlier research has also shown that *psychological autonomy* can best be assessed by asking youth whether their parents use love withdrawal or excessive guilt to control their behavior. We used proven questions developed by others to measure psychological autonomy.

We also gathered anecdotal information from the youth in the study through open-ended questions. An example is, "What have been the strongest pressures in your life to live the standards of the Church?" The question was repeated asking the youth to identify pressures to *not* live the standards. Also, several hundred BYU students were surveyed with open-ended questions concerning the challenges they had faced as teenagers, how they had dealt with those challenges, and what role their religious values and families had played in helping them resist peer pressure and temptation. The two or three extra years of maturity and hindsight allowed these young adults to provide us with some very thoughtful insights into the power of friends, faith, and family.

We analyzed the information contained in the surveys in two main ways. First, the delinquency, peer influence, religiosity, and family characteristics of the youth in the three different regions were compared. Statistical significance means that a difference in delinquency between young men and young women did not occur by chance. In other words, such a difference will appear in other studies comparing young men's and young women's delinquency.

Second, the model shown in figure 1—including peer influence, religiosity, and family characteristics—was tested using a sophisticated statistical procedure called structure equation analysis (LISREL). This type of analysis first confirmed whether the questions we asked in the questionnaire were appropriate indicators of the factors or characteristics in the model. In other words, did the questions we asked about delinquency really measure delinquent behavior? Once it was determined that the questionnaire items did indeed assess peer, religious, and family characteristics, then the procedure calculated the "causal" relationships between peer pressure, religiosity, family characteristics, and delinquency. Or in other words, this allowed us to better understand to what degree these other characteristics and traits actually cause or deter delinquency.

From all of this—the statistical findings, the comments of the young people, and our own experiences as parents and Church leaders—comes an in-depth picture of the challenges faced by LDS youth. In this book we attempt the task of mixing social science findings, religious principles, prophetic statements, and our own experiences to offer suggestions about raising righteous teens. At times we will move beyond a strict interpretation of our data and make some inferences, or perhaps leaps of faith. We did not discover in the course of our research some new philosophy or parenting practice that will protect our youth from evil. There is no single way to raise children that will guarantee they will grow up to be faithful, productive members of society. But we are convinced that there are some general principles that parents can adapt to their individual children that will help them resist temptation and assist them in their personal struggles to become competent adults.

Unfortunately we cannot *isolate* our youth from all wickedness, but the family and the gospel provide a means whereby we can *insulate* them. As Elder M. Russell Ballard declared, "The home and family have vital roles in cultivating and developing personal faith and testimony."

The family is the basic unit of society; the best place for individuals to build faith and strong testimonies is in righteous homes filled with love. Love for our Heavenly Father and his Son Jesus Christ is greatly enhanced when the gospel is taught and lived in the home. True principles of eternal life are embedded in the hearts and souls of young and old alike when scriptures are read and discussed, when prayers are offered morning and night, and where reverence for God and obedience to Him are modeled in everyday conduct. Just as the best meals are home cooked, the most nourishing gospel instruction takes place at home. Strong faithful families have the best opportunity to produce strong faithful members of the Church. ("Feasting at the Lord's Table," *Ensign,* May 1996, p. 81.)

**Figure 1**

**Model with Peer Influences, Religiosity, and Family Characteristics Predicting Delinquency**

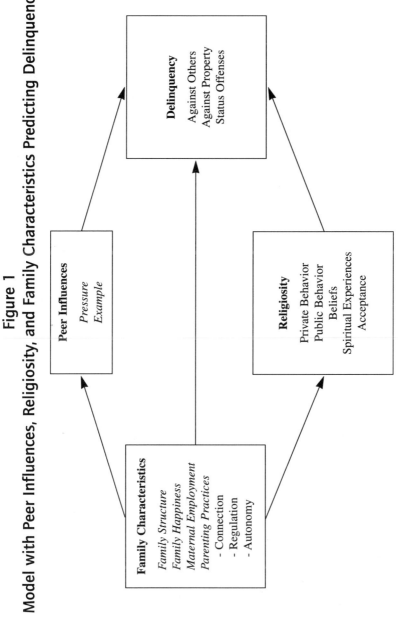

# 2

# HOW ARE THE "SATURDAY'S WARRIORS" DOING?

## GREAT NEWS, GOOD NEWS, AND NOT-SO-GOOD NEWS

"Never has the Church had a more choice group of young people than at present," President Ezra Taft Benson declared, "and Satan is well aware of who they are. He is doing everything in his power to thwart them in their destiny. He knows that they have been sent to earth in this crucial period of the world's history to build the king- dom of God and establish Zion in preparation for the second coming of the Lord Jesus Christ. Yes, our youth have an awesome challenge." (*The Teachings of Ezra Taft Benson,* pp. 562–63.) These youth, as President Benson and other prophets have testified, have been re- served to come forth in these difficult times. These valiant spirits who have been reserved to come forth at this time have been affec- tionately labeled by a popular LDS musical as "Saturday's Warriors." They are like Helaman's 2,000 stripling warriors, but instead of fighting physical battles, the stripling warriors of today have come forth in the Saturday of the world's history to wage spiritual warfare against the many forces of evil. Iniquity abounds as Lucifer's desperate "last gasp" evil efforts increase and the need for righteous and worthy spirits to carry forth God's purposes and designs increases proportionately. So, how are these Saturday's warriors—these choice spirit sons and daughters of God, the nobility of heaven who have been kept in the spirit world to come forth in the last days—doing in their personal lives in meeting the challenges and temptations they face? How are they doing in preparing to achieve their divine destiny? The results of our study helped us to get a better picture of how these modern-day stripling warriors are accomplishing their lofty goals. Among LDS youth today, we discovered that there is great news and some not-so-good news. Each kind of news—even when some of the things we discover are disconcerting—helps us to better understand how the youth are faring and what we can do to more adequately nurture their spiritual development so they can fulfill their foreordained missions.

## The Great News:
## National Comparisons

First, the great news. The LDS teenagers we surveyed reported significantly lower levels of delinquency than that of other youth in the nation. Each year *Monitoring the Future* conducts a large survey of high school seniors across the nation. Table 2.1 clearly illustrates the substantial differences between LDS seniors and this national sample of high school seniors. Nationally, over 80 percent of high school seniors have ever experimented with alcohol, while only slightly more than 20 percent of LDS seniors reported having ever used alcohol. Similar dramatic differences are observed in teen sexual behavior. The national average for premarital sexual intercourse is over 70 percent, as compared to only about 15 percent of LDS seniors. Several recent national publications have reported even higher

# Table 2.1

## Delinquent Behavior of LDS High School Seniors as Compared to High School Seniors Nationally

### Percent Who Have "Ever Done" in Lifetime

| Delinquent Activity | Youth in Nation | | LDS Youth in East Coast | | LDS Youth in Pacific Northwest | | LDS Youth in Utah County | |
|---|---|---|---|---|---|---|---|---|
| | Males (N=7708) | Females (N=8310) | Males (N=120) | Females (N=147) | Males (N=66) | Females (N=97) | Males (N=82) | Females (N=108) |
| Smoked cigarettes[1] | 64% | 60% | 22% | 23% | 25% | 19% | 28% | 8% |
| Used smokeless tobacco[1] | 51% | 12% | 11% | 3% | 14% | 5% | 16% | 3% |
| Drank alcoholic beverages[1] | 81% | 80% | 23% | 23% | 15% | 20% | 28% | 16% |
| Been drunk or very high on alcohol[1] | 63% | 59% | 18% | 14% | 12% | 13% | 19% | 9% |
| Used marijuana[1] | 39% | 31% | 9% | 8% | 10% | 5% | 18% | 7% |
| Used cocaine[1] | 8% | 5% | 2% | 1% | 4% | 0% | 5% | 0% |
| Had sexual intercourse (1989)[2] | 73% | 56% | 10% | 22% | 6% | 18% | 14% | 9% |
| Been suspended or expelled from school[1] | 31% | 16% | 20% | 7% | 23% | 4% | 21% | 6% |

[1] Johnston, L. D., Bachman, J. G., & O'Malley, P. M. (1993). *Monitoring the Future*, Ann Arbor, MI: Survey Research Center, Institute for Social Research, University of Michigan, pp. 250, 277.
[2] Benson, P. L. (1990). *The Troubled Journey: A Portrait of 6th-12th Grade Youth*. Minneapolis, MN: Search Institute, p. 54.

rates of promiscuity among high school students in the United States than those reported in our table. Obviously, LDS youth in our study look even better when compared against these results.

The *Monitoring the Future* study also asks each sample of high school seniors if they belong to a church, and, if they do, to which denomination. We purchased the data set for 1994 and compared the use of illicit drugs in general and marijuana in particular by seniors belonging to different religious denominations. Fortunately for such a comparison, over 300 LDS seniors were included in the 1994 study. The results, presented in table 2.2, show that LDS seniors have the lowest rate of both illicit drug and marijuana use. This also is great news concerning the youth of the Church. Interestingly, the highest rates of drug use were reported by those seniors with *no* religious affiliation.

### Table 2.2
### Comparison of Illicit Drug Use of National High School Seniors by Religious Denomination[1]

| Religious Preference (N) | Illicit Drug Use | |
|---|---|---|
| | Illicit Drugs | Marijuana Only |
| LDS (303) | 31.1% | 9.4% |
| Other Protestant (544) | 36.6% | 11.0% |
| Methodist (1,119) | 38.4% | 11.1% |
| Baptist (3,454) | 38.8% | 17.4% |
| Other religions (1,119) | 40.0% | 13.0% |
| Lutheran (704) | 41.7% | 15.5% |
| Roman Catholic (3,917) | 44.9% | 16.9% |
| Church of Christ (927) | 45.2% | 18.8% |
| Presbyterian (448) | 45.3% | 21.4% |
| Jewish (176) | 48.4% | 22.1% |
| None (2,558) | 53.6% | 17.7% |

[1] Johnston, L. D., Bachman, J. G., & O'Malley, P. M. (1993). *Monitoring the Future,* Ann Arbor, MI: Survey Research Center, Institute for Social Research, University of Michigan, pp. 250, 277.

# The Not-So-Good News: Delinquency Among LDS Youth

Although the LDS teens are less delinquent than their national peers, they do make mistakes and do engage in behaviors that are at odds with the standards of the Church and principles of the gospel. While this is the not-so-good news, it should not totally surprise us since neither any of us nor any of our children will go through life without sinning. The percentages of LDS youth who have ever engaged in various delinquent activities are presented in table 2.3. These percentages are for all of the ninth through twelfth grade teens in the three samples, not just the seniors. It was discouraging to discover that nearly 20 percent admitted they had cursed or swore at their parents, while 10 percent acknowledged having shoved or hit their mother or father. Surprisingly, the young women in the study revealed they abused their parents as often as the young men. Fighting and beating up other youth had been participated in by about a fourth of the young men and less than 10 percent of the young women.

Approximately a third of the youth in the study admitted to having shoplifted and over 70 percent reported they have cheated on tests in school. Over half of the young men and a third of the young women admitted they had trespassed on someone's property, and about a fourth of the young men and a little over 10 percent of the young women have vandalized others' property.

About a fourth of the youth, both young men and women, have tried smoking cigarettes and drinking beer, wine, or hard liquor. Marijuana experimentation has occurred among 7 or 8 percent of the youth. Significantly more young men than young women, slightly under half of those surveyed, have read and watched pornographic material. Nearly 30 percent of both young men and women reported having engaged in petting, while around 9 percent have experienced sexual intercourse. This is not-so-good news.

29

We asked the youth in our study, "What has been the strongest temptation in your life to not live the standards of the gospel?" These Latter-day Saint teens reported both strong social and personal desires or drives to engage in these kinds of inappropriate activities. Based on these comments we can see why some delinquent behaviors had higher levels of participation than others. For example, nearly one-quarter of the youth reported that their most difficult challenge was compromising personal integrity, such as lying, stealing, or cheating in school. *"I think cheating is a hard pressure to deal with,"* one of the teens wrote, *"because everyone around you is doing it and they think it's not that big a deal. That makes it extra hard to resist."* Several youth justified cheating because "everyone does it" and "if I don't I will be handicapped in competing for grades and ultimately university admission." Another youth reported that lying was his biggest challenge. *"I lie to my parents about where I am going and what I am going to do, so they will let me go. If I don't I won't be able to go with my friends and I'll be stuck home with my parents."* Being stuck home with parents is a fate worse than death to most teenagers.

Temptation to break the Word of Wisdom was cited by nearly the same number of the teens as their greatest challenge. *"I have a lot of pressure by people wanting me to drink and do drugs (pot),"* one young lady reported. Many, many others made similar comments about not only the verbal pressure to drink or use drugs they faced but also the unspoken, social pressure they felt because of the open availability of such substances. *"Pressure to 'party' is the worst,"* another reported. *"It is viewed as 'cool' to get drunk and to smoke. It is so socially acceptable, and 'everyone' seems to be doing it."* Another wrote: *"All of my friends go to parties and drink alcohol and use drugs most every weekend. They always ask me why I never come. 'They are so fun,' they say. Sometimes I feel left out, but most of the time I have fun without using those things."* Another young man reported that his friends were the athletes from school, who *"hung out together and partied."* He said, *"There was always alcohol being served and often drugs with which to experiment if one desired."*

Threats to personal purity—pornography, petting, and sexual intercourse—was the *most often cited* pressure facing LDS teens both in Utah and outside of Utah. Nearly 40 percent of them identified immorality as the greatest pressure they are facing in their personal lives. Not only do the comments from the youth but also the results presented in table 2.3 confirm what President Ezra Taft Benson declared: "The plaguing sin of this generation is sexual immorality. This, the Prophet Joseph said, would be the source of more temptations, more buffetings, and more difficulties for the elders [and sisters] of Israel than any other." (*The Teachings of Ezra Taft Benson*, p. 277.) The young people had a lot to say about the challenge to be morally clean in a wicked world. One young man got his point across rather emphatically, if not humorously, when he reported on his greatest challenge: *"Women kindle the passions. Women, women, women, women, women. Did I mention women?"* Some of the many other insightful and heartfelt comments of the teens include the following:

> *The strongest pressure in my life has been boys (sex). Satan is so strong! I wish so badly that I could go back and undo some of the things I have done. Especially losing my virginity and doing it more than once. But it seems like when I finally realize what I've done, Satan finds a way to make it look like it's not that bad.*

> *The strongest thing that I have faced is premarital sex. What a difficult thing! But even though I have done this, it makes me feel good to know that I can fully repent of this sin, that the Lord will forgive me and I can forgive myself.*

> *I think a lot of kids like me get sucked into the trap of immorality almost innocently and ignorantly. I was probably in 6th or 7th grade*

31

*when I got into pornography pretty heavily. What started out as a curiosity soon became a bad habit. It always led to other things. I kinda got sucked into immorality by accident, but I have had to battle this thing for years.*

Many of the young people stated that the temptations they face to be immoral are heightened by the media to which they are exposed continually. *"Bad movies,"* one student identified as the greatest pressure. *"The media sucks you in if you are not careful. Satan is trying very hard by pushing premarital sexual activities."* Many of the teens reported that, while they would never go to R-rated movies in theaters, they feel it is not so bad to watch the same movies at "video parties" at home or at friends' houses. *"My biggest struggle has been to keep my mind clean,"* one of the teens stated, *"because TV and everything is getting so bad now. I have learned that it's just much better to not watch any television."* Hundreds of comments of the young people in our study shared their feelings of being surrounded by subtle, as well as not so subtle, messages that immorality is really not so bad. These comments confirm the apostolic warning given by Elder Boyd K. Packer in general conference:

> The rapid, sweeping deterioration of values is characterized by a preoccupation—even an obsession—with the procreative act. Abstinence before marriage and fidelity within it are openly scoffed at—marriage and parenthood ridiculed as burdensome, unnecessary. Modesty, a virtue of a refined individual or society, is all but gone. . . .
>
> With ever fewer exceptions, what we see and read and hear have the mating act as a central theme. Censorship is forced offstage as a violation of individual freedom.
>
> That which should be absolutely private is disrobed and acted out on center stage. In the shadows backstage are addiction, pornography, perversion, infidelity, abortion, and—the saddest of them

all—incest and molestation. In company with them now is a plague of biblical proportion. All of them are on the increase. . . .

God grant that we will come to our senses and protect our moral environment from this mist of darkness which deepens day by day. The fate of all humanity hangs precariously in the balance. (In Conference Report, April 1992, pp. 91–95.)

We were quite surprised to discover that significantly more young women than young men on the East Coast and in the Pacific Northwest are sexually experienced (see table 2.3). This gender gap widens with age, as 22 percent of high school senior girls in those two regions have had sexual intercourse compared to only 10 percent of the senior boys! This finding caught us off guard since nationally boys tend to initiate sexual activity at an earlier age than young women and are more sexually active. As can be seen in the table, Utah County youths' sexual activity reflects this national trend. This high vulnerability of LDS young women living in the mission field caused us to puzzle over what is happening to them.

Although we cannot state for sure because we did not ask questions about dating, we think that it has to do with LDS young women in the mission field dating older, non-LDS young men who do not share the same values of morality. Usually LDS young men do not date early because they do not have their driver's license. In addition, they would never think of dating an older young woman (someone in a higher grade), so often they wait even a little longer for a given young woman to also turn sixteen before they seek their first date. On the other hand, 16-year-old LDS young women may be initiated into dating by older boys, who ofttimes are sexually active. It seems to us that the temptation, and even pressure, to be immoral is intensified when dating those who are not of our faith who may not share our values regarding chastity. The danger of dating non-LDS youth is seen in the dramatic differences between premarital

# Table 2.3
## Percent of LDS Youth Who Have Committed Offenses Against Others, Against Property, and Status Offenses, by Sex and Region

|  | *Males* | | | *Females* | | |
|---|---|---|---|---|---|---|
|  | East Coast (N=636) | West Coast (N=261) | Utah Valley (N=460) | East Coast (N=754) | West Coast (N=370) | Utah Valley (N=598) |
| **Offenses Against Others** | | | | | | |
| Cursed or swore at a parent | 19% | 19% | 21% | 21% | 20% | 20% |
| Pushed, shoved, or hit a parent | 10 | 12 | 9 | 14 | 10 | 8 |
| Openly defied school teacher/official | 36 | 34 | 27 | 26 | 22 | 18 |
| Been suspended or expelled from school | 20 | 19 | 13 | 6 | 7 | 5 |
| Called on telephone to threaten/bother | 21 | 32 | 27 | 23 | 27 | 27 |
| Picked on kids/made fun of/called names | 52 | 52 | 41 | 43 | 34 | 31 |
| Physically beat up other kids | 25 | 25 | 19 | 8 | 6 | 5 |
| Been in a gang fight | 8 | 6 | 6 | 2 | 3 | 2 |
| Forced or pressured sexual activities | 5 | 6 | 6 | 5 | 3 | 4 |
| **Offenses Against Property** | | | | | | |
| Took something from a store without paying for it | 33% | 39% | 34% | 20% | 22% | 19% |
| Stole anything worth between $5 and $50 | 18 | 22 | 19 | 10 | 12 | 10 |
| Stole anything less than $5 | 37 | 40 | 33 | 22 | 21 | 19 |
| Went onto someone's property without permission | 53 | 51 | 51 | 34 | 34 | 37 |
| Purposely ruined/damaged property or possessions | 26 | 29 | 29 | 12 | 11 | 13 |
| Took car or motor vehicle without owner's permission | 8 | 10 | 12 | 6 | 8 | 12 |
| **Status Offenses** | | | | | | |
| Smoked cigarettes | 24% | 18% | 17% | 24% | 19% | 9% |
| Used "smokeless" or chewing tobacco | 12 | 10 | 10 | 3 | 5 | 2 |
| Drank alcoholic beverages (beer, wine, liquor) | 24 | 13 | 16 | 27 | 19 | 13 |
| Used marijuana ("grass," "pot") | 7 | 8 | 8 | 5 | 9 | 4 |
| Been drunk or high on drugs | 12 | 8 | 8 | 13 | 11 | 7 |
| Run away from home | 12 | 10 | 13 | 13 | 13 | 12 |
| Cheated on a test | 70 | 66 | 69 | 73 | 71 | 65 |
| Read sexually explicit or pornographic books or magazines | 46 | 48 | 37 | 20 | 16 | 11 |
| Watched sexually explicit movies or TV | 42 | 46 | 39 | 27 | 21 | 16 |
| Been involved in heavy petting | 29 | 23 | 19 | 32 | 29 | 19 |
| Had sexual intercourse | 7 | 6 | 6 | 12 | 9 | 5 |

sex among the national sample of seniors and the LDS seniors reported in table 2.1.

The relationship between early dating, or even pairing off, with those who do not share our value system and immorality was identified by President Spencer W. Kimball, who counseled young people not to date before sixteen and to be extremely careful in their dating practices. He declared:

> Early dating increases temptation. A vicious, destructive, social pattern of early steady dating must be changed. . . .
>
> It is my considered feeling, having had some experience in interviewing youth, that the change of this one pattern of social activities of our youth would immediately eliminate a majority of the sins of our young folks. (*The Teachings of Spencer W. Kimball* [Salt Lake City: Bookcraft, 1982], pp. 287–88.)
>
> Early dating—especially early steady dating—brings numerous problems—much heartache and numerous disasters. The early date ofttimes develops into the steady date; the steady date frequently brings on early marriages. . . .
>
> Steady dating is the source of much evil. The casual relationship grows rapidly into intimacies, develops heavy temptations, and stirs passions far beyond the ability of most of our young people to cope with. Nearly 40 percent of our unwed mothers are between fifteen and nineteen years of age. Even our finest young people will find difficulty in withstanding for a long period the temptations of intimate, frequent association. And the best young men and young women may be overwhelmed and led down the path of the sins of necking, petting, fornication, and other detestable and loathsome perversions and practices. (*The Teachings of Spencer W. Kimball,* p. 289.)

Do not take the chance of dating nonmembers, or members who are untrained and faithless. A girl may say, "Oh I do not intend to marry this person. It is just a 'fun' date." But one cannot afford to take a chance on falling in love with someone who may never accept the gospel. (*The Teachings of Spencer W. Kimball,* p. 300.)

Helpfully, there were some comments from the young people in our studies that offer suggestions about how to cope with the pervasive pressures to be immoral. In their responses to open-ended questions, scores of the teens stated that they wished their parents would be more open with them about the physical and emotional changes they are experiencing as they mature sexually. Many expressed a need for specific guidance, as well as support and understanding of the pressures teens face concerning their sexuality. Some teens said they felt their parents were too bashful or embarrassed to have discussions on such a sensitive topic. They wanted and needed to be able to talk with their parents, not just be lectured to or have their feelings ignored by them. This confirms a caution given to Latter-day Saint parents by President Ezra Taft Benson:

> Sexual immorality is a viper that is striking not only in the world, but in the Church today. Not to admit it is to be dangerously complacent or is like putting one's head in the sand. . . .
>
> Parents should give their children specific instructions on chastity at an early age, both for their physical and moral protection. (*The Teachings of Ezra Taft Benson,* pp. 278–79.)

Teach children gospel principles. Teach them it pays to be good. Teach them there is no safety in sin. Teach them a love for the gospel of Jesus Christ and a testimony of its divinity. Teach your sons and daughters modesty and teach them to respect manhood and womanhood. Teach your children sexual purity, proper dating standards, temple marriage, missionary service, and the importance of accepting and magnifying Church callings. Teach them a love for work and the value of a good education. Teach them the importance of the right kind of entertainment, including appropriate movies,

videos, music, books, and magazines. Discuss the evils of pornography and drugs and teach them the value of living a clean life.
(*The Teachings of Ezra Taft Benson,* p. 517.)

The youth themselves yearn to have the kind of spiritual yet
practical guidance of which President Benson is speaking. When we
asked the young adults in our follow-up study, "What, if anything, do
you wish your parents would have done differently or not done as
you were growing up to better help you meet the challenges faced by
LDS teenagers today?" we received a loud cry for information about
sexuality and morality. Here are but a few:

*I wish they would have educated me at an earlier age about sex and
drugs—maybe even by the 5th grade.*

*I wish they would have talked more openly about hard issues like
sex, AIDS, homosexuality, drugs, abortion, etc. Rather than talk
down to me I would have liked them to talk through these things
with me.*

*I wish they would have taught me more specifically about morality
very early on, and continued to watch me and warn me about
things. I think a lot of times just because I didn't have a serious girlfriend they figured I was clean, but I was still facing other challenges.*

*Mom didn't teach us anything about the opposite sex, and because
my dad was gone, I knew nothing about my own body. I wish I
would have been taught some form of sex education. Because I knew
so little, I felt I had to explore and find out for myself and sometimes
that led to problems.*

*I wish that I would have been better taught about moral transgres-
sion and the consequences that come with giving into temptation.*

*I wish my parents would have shared with us some of their own challenges and temptations they faced when they were young and how they were able to resist those pressures.*

*My parents never talked about morality issues. I think they felt uncomfortable discussing it or didn't know how to bring it up, and therefore I never knew how to approach them with my questions and concerns. I wish they would have been more open.*

*The most important thing they could have done would be to have listened more when I wanted to talk about moral challenges, and judged less. I just wanted someone to understand what I was feeling, but instead whenever I would even say anything about sex or morality issues they would "freak out" and think I was going to hell.*

Our experiences as bishops and youth leaders have convinced us that some LDS parents are neglecting the training of their children concerning their sexuality. We frequently heard the young people ask, "What counts as petting?" "What is masturbation?" and "Where is the boundary between chastity and immorality?" Satan and his followers have justified immoral behavior in teens' eyes in ways that would shock their parents. For example, many times young people have asked us whether oral sex violates the law of chastity! The belief that they can participate in oral sex and still be worthy to be married in the temple is accepted by a sizable number of young people in the Church.

Also, we have been amazed with the casualness with which LDS young people participate in sexual behavior. Many youth reported that they would ride home from work with a co-worker and end up in heavy petting or having sex. They had never dated, there was no built-up passion, no thought of marriage, yet they crossed the line to immoral behavior. Sex at times seemed to be a rather trivial activity, of no real consequence. Some preteens and very early teens experiment with sex among their friends long before they are of dating age. As President Benson counseled, greater guidance about what it means to be morally clean and better teaching of the importance of avoiding "anything like unto it" should come from parents in a direct yet loving way. We as parents cannot afford to be "bashful" or "shy away" from talking about chastity in specific terms, though guided by the promptings of the Spirit, for Satan is not bashful or tentative in his all-out bombardment of the youth.

In an article entitled, "What Kids *Really* Need from Mom," noted author and psychologist, Dr. Joyce Brothers, wrote that children need their mothers (and certainly fathers) to engage in what she characterized as taboo talk.

> We live in a dangerous world where kids are exposed to drugs, alcohol and sex at ever-younger ages. Some mothers fear that talking about such taboo activities sanctions them. The opposite is true. A 1994 study of fifth- and seventh-graders in Southern California, for instance, found that children who have honest discussions with their parents are less likely to use drugs and alcohol.
>
> Moms can be especially good at talking to kids about these sensitive topics. First, familiarize yourself with the facts about the issue, be it drugs, drinking or teen sex. Then ask your children what they know: kids as young as six or seven may have heard stories on the playground or seen something on TV. Point out that you're talking about the issue so your children understand its dangers, not because you don't trust them. Let them know that you're willing to answer any questions or discuss their worries. (In *Readers Digest,* Jan. 1998, p. 38.)

Parents need to be more aware of and empathetic to the challenges and temptations facing youth today and be willing to lovingly teach them not only the standards of the gospel but also the very real blessings that come with being pure. This communication and instruction can only occur in a spiritually and emotionally supportive environment. In a subsequent chapter we will discuss in detail how parents can foster this family communication where such guidance can be lovingly given and received.

## It's Not Where You Live That Counts— It's What You Do!

One of the most important findings of this study is that it appears that there is little difference in the behavior of LDS youth and their families regardless of the region where they live. If the religious ecology theory were correct, then LDS teenagers from the Pacific Northwest and the East Coast would be significantly more delinquent than their peers in Utah. That just isn't the case. We were amazed how similar the youth and their families were in so many ways. The frequency of church attendance, gospel beliefs, two-parent families, family prayer, family home evening, and the levels of family connectedness, regulation, and psychological autonomy were for all practical purposes identical. A strong LDS family is a strong LDS family regardless of where it resides. This should be considered as really good news! The only exception was that the peer pressure to participate in delinquent activities, especially behaviors not generally frowned upon in society such as drinking and premarital sex, was higher among LDS youth living in the mission field. It is important to note that the higher level of peer pressure and more delinquent friends is *not* associated with more delinquency among the LDS youth.

The upshot of this somewhat surprising finding is that parents need not unduly worry about the many evil influences surrounding their children in their particular community or wonder if a wayward teen might not have strayed from the gospel had they lived somewhere else. Parents need not long for a "spiritual Shangri-la" in which to raise their children. Unfortunately we don't have such a place, but fortunately we don't need one. The reality is that good kids can turn bad just as easily in Utah as anywhere else and that spiritually strong and faithful youth can survive and even prosper in a small branch of the Church or in a school with no other LDS kids. The oft-repeated arguments concerning whether it is better to raise your children in the "mission field" or in the "heart of Mormondom" seem to be moot. Zion is as much, if not more, a spiritual condition than a geographical location (see D&C 97:21). The roots of faith and testimony that will give strength to young people can go down deeply in any of the soil of the world. It is certainly good news to know that it doesn't seem to be so much where a family lives that determines if their teenagers will be able to resist temptations and avoid delinquency and immorality as much as what happens within the walls of that home and within the heart and soul of that youth.

# The Wayward Teen:
# Some Reasons Why

The reader will recall that the second objective of our study was to test a causal model of delinquency among LDS youth that included peer influences, religiosity, and family characteristics (see figure 1). The results are presented in figure 2. The first lesson learned from this statistical model is that peer pressure has the strongest relationship with delinquency. The beta coefficient of .416 indicates that the greater the pressure from friends to participate in delinquency, the greater the delinquency of the youth. Betas vary from 1.0, which indicates a perfect relationship between a factor such as peer pressure and delinquency, to 00.0, which indicates no relationship at all. Statisticians generally agree that in structural equation modeling, a beta coefficient above .05 indicates a statistically significant relationship and a beta above .10 indicates a substantive relationship. Thus a beta of

.416 reveals a strong relationship between peer pressure and delinquency. Peer example, the proportion of friends who engage in delinquent activities, also made an independent contribution (beta =.144) to explaining why LDS youth engage in behaviors that are at odds with the standards of the gospel. Even though their friends may not pressure them, if those friends nonetheless participate in delinquent activities, then LDS youth tend to join them.

Perhaps the most important finding to emerge from the study is that religiosity, independent of peer influences, does indeed have a significant effect on the behavior of LDS teenagers. To test the model, we combined the five dimensions of religiosity—belief, public behavior, private behavior, spiritual experience, and feelings of belonging in the ward—into an overall religiosity score. Religiosity is related to the avoidance of delinquency, as revealed by the -.191 beta. The minus sign means that LDS youth who believe gospel truths, attend their meetings, pray, read the scriptures, and feel welcome in their ward, participate in less delinquent behavior.

## Figure 2.1
## Theoretical Model of Delinquency

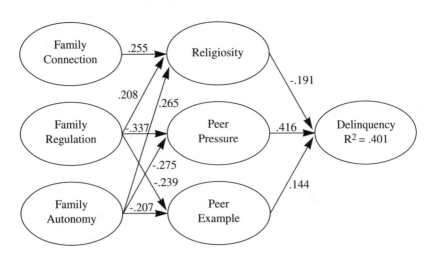

Rather interesting findings emerged out of the test of the model concerning family influence. First, the two family characteristics—single-parent versus two-parent family and having a mother who is employed outside the home—dropped out of the model as insignificant. In other words, peers, religiosity, and the three parenting practices are so much more important that these two family characteristics do not make an independent contribution to understanding delinquency. Second, previous research has been mixed as to whether the family has a *direct* relationship to delinquency. For the youth in our samples, none of the family characteristics have a direct link to delinquency. This is not to say the family is not important in guiding youth to remain on the straight and narrow. Rather, as can be seen in figure 2, the three parenting practices have powerful *indirect* effects on delinquency. Connection with parents is strongly related to religiosity (beta=.255), which in turn is negatively related to delinquent behavior. In other words, youth who feel connected to their parents have stronger religious beliefs and practices, which in turn reduce violation of gospel principles and the law. Regulation is significantly related to religiosity (beta =.208) and also negatively related to peer pressure (beta =-.337) and peer example (beta=-.239), all three of which are linked to delinquency. Psychological autonomy is also related to religiosity, peer pressures, and peer examples, and thus has a strong indirect effect on delinquency. These findings indicate that parents who are connected with their teens, who regulate their behavior, and who grant them psychological autonomy have a strong effect on the selection of friends, on their resistance to their pressures to sin, and on the internalization of religious values and principles, all of which in turn influence delinquency.

For the statistically minded, the $R^2$ =.401 in figure 2 reveals that peer influences, religious principles, and the three parenting practices account for 40 percent of the delinquent behavior reported by the youth. The other 60 percent is accounted for by other unknown influences and by error in measuring delinquency, peer influences, religiosity, and family processes with our questionnaire.

In summary, we confirmed for LDS youth what many have discovered before—that peers are the single most important influence affecting youth in choosing to engage in immoral or illegal activities. The results clearly demonstrate that LDS youth do internalize religious beliefs, values, and principles that guide their behavior. Finally, we confirm what the Church leaders have often said: the family does make a difference in the lives of teenagers, including helping them in obeying Church standards and the laws of the land.

Because these three influences—friends, church, and family—do make a difference in the lives of teenagers by helping them avoid sin and delinquency, we will discuss in the chapters that follow what parents can do to help their children select good friends and how to maximize positive peer influences and to minimize negative ones. We will also offer suggestions of things parents can do to assist youth to internalize the gospel and to develop a strong testimony, which is translated into righteous living. Finally, we will present suggestions about what parents can do to foster connectedness with their teenage children, to appropriately regulate their behavior, and to allow teens the necessary psychological autonomy.

# 3

# THE POWER OF PEERS
## For Good or Evil

The teenage years bring with them a substantial need to belong or fit in with friendship groups. Although people of all ages desire friends—those whose company we enjoy, who encourage us to succeed, and who commiserate with us during the hard times—these desires assume greater importance for adolescents. As teenagers expand their social world beyond their family, friends assume even more eminence in their lives. This need for acceptance by friends was obvious in the youths' responses to the question, "What has been the greatest pressure in your life *to live* the standards of the Church?" The question was repeated for "*not to live* the standards." Interestingly, friends topped *both* lists. They were identified as the strongest influence to live as well as the strongest influence not to live LDS standards. The comments highlighted, sometimes painfully, teens' desire to be accepted within the football team, the debate club, the honor society, the high school band, or just a group of friends that hang out together. In addition, the students' comments illustrate how friends can be both an influence to do good or to lead youth away from gospel principles into wicked and worldly practices.

*My biggest pressure to not live the standards of the Church is definitely my friends. I don't know what it is, but I think it is a desire to fit in or be "popular." The problem is I'm a little bit shy and so when I'm around my friends I feel I have to make them like me and sometimes I do things I know are wrong. But if I don't do these things, I am rejected and feel isolated.*

*Pressures for me have been from wanting to fit in, from seeing my friends do things which aren't the best and from not wanting to be made fun of. I think this makes it hard for me to fully understand what's right and wrong and so I sometimes do things I regret later.*

*I have had friends in the past who pressured for bad. And I long to be accepted!!*

*Pressures against keeping the standards have been from wanting to fit in, seeing my friends do things which maybe are not the best, and not wanting to be made fun of, wanting to have friends. I think sometimes I don't fully understand what's right and wrong in situations when it's not obvious.*

Two major themes leaped out at us from the many written comments of the youth about the role of friends in their lives. First, the phrase "fit in" frequently appeared. LDS young people want very much to be accepted by those they associate with in school, church, and neighborhood. Second, the desire to fit in or to be popular is so strong that many youth compromise their standards in an effort to belong. For example, in our years of service in the Church working with youth, we have encountered numerous young women who participated in petting and other sexual activities not because of passion but rather because they were desperate for confirmation that they are attractive and acceptable or because they felt some obligation to please a boyfriend. Mary Pipher's bestselling book, *Reviving Ophelia* (New York: Ballantine Books, 1995), discusses the painful identity crisis many young women in American society experience as they pass from childhood into adulthood.

Girls become "female impersonators" who fit their whole selves into small, crowded spaces. Vibrant, confident girls become shy, doubting young women. Girls stop thinking "Who am I? What do I want?" and start thinking "What must I do to please others?"

Pipher suggests that, just like Shakespeare's Ophelia, adolescent girls' sense of identity is defined in terms of their attachment to others. Young women are so desperate to make themselves attractive to young men that they develop eating disorders trying to attain the socially acceptable figure and will violate their own personal standards when asked. When young women feel they have failed in their efforts to belong, many fall prey to depression, alcohol and drug use, self-mutilation, and even suicide.

Although the overwhelming need to belong seems to be stronger among young women, young men experience the same feelings with many of the same problems. If parents want to help their teenage children in their quest for adulthood, they must recognize the powerful desire youth have to be accepted by their peers.

The influence of friends—for good or bad—comes in two different ways. First, friends impact each other through their example. If a young man or young woman's friends are drinking and give the appearance of having fun and being cool, the LDS youth may join them. The youth feel that joining in the inappropriate behavior will somehow make others like them more. A second way friends influence youth is through actual pressure. Pressure may range from subtle encouragement such as "Try it, you'll like it," to providing the opportunity to sin by offering a drink or a smoke from a marijuana cigarette, to hard-to-ignore challenges of being "chicken," "afraid," or "a mommy's boy." This latter type of pressure is extremely difficult for youth to withstand as, in addition to threatening their fitting in, it also challenges their claim to adulthood.

Peer influences obviously may change a youth's behavior. A

young man or young woman may smoke marijuana, drink alcohol, skip school, shoplift from a department store, or engage in sexual activities because of a desire to join with friends or because friends pressured him or her to do so. A second influence of friends that was alluded to in the written comments is a blurring of perceptions of right or wrong. Several youth wrote how hanging out with bad friends confused their sense of what was sin.

A recent network television newsmagazine program reported a replication of a famous psychology experiment about how peers influence the perceptions of college students. Solomon Asch, a Harvard psychologist, originally conducted the study in the 1950s. He asked unsuspecting students to match the length of a line drawn on a card to three lines drawn on another card. The match was obvious and could be correctly identified by almost anyone over 99 percent of the time. Peer pressure was introduced by having trained students who knew what was going on with the experiment purposely select an incorrect line. The number of these students was varied and Asch discovered that seven or eight produced the strongest peer pressure. Thus the unsuspecting subject and seven trained students who were "in on the fix" were seated around a table. One by one each of the confederates, whom the subject thought were merely fellow students, purposely selected the wrong line. The naive subject was placed next to last so that seven peers chose the incorrect line ahead of him or her. It was discovered that one-third of the young people in the experiment went along with the group and selected the same incorrect line almost immediately. Others held out a little longer and very few continued to select the correct answer every round. Interestingly, young people today are just as susceptible to peer pressures as the youth of the fifties. Why the subjects followed the crowd can't be determined. Some may have simply "gone along to get along." They knew the selection was wrong, but they did it because they did not want to stand out as different. Several of the subjects interviewed after the experiment said that they chose the line everyone else did because they were "afraid of sticking out like a sore thumb." On the other hand, some may have actually had their perception altered so that they came to believe the incorrect was correct. This psychological phenomenon coincides with what several LDS youth in our study stated about how their friends caused them to lose the ability to recognize right from wrong.

## Peer Influences Experienced by LDS Teenagers

We expected LDS youth living in the mission field to experience greater peer pressure than teens living in Utah in regards to committing delinquent activities, especially status or victimless offenses like drinking and premarital sex. These expectations were based on the observation that the youth living along the East Coast and in the Pacific Northwest have many more nonmember friends who do not hold the same values and who are not trying to live the same standards. We didn't ask the East Coast teenagers how many of their friends were members of the Church, but the difference between the mission field and Utah is evident in the reports of the youth in the Pacific Northwest and those in Utah. Only 30 percent of the LDS teens in the Pacific Northwest reported that "most" or "all" of their *close* friends were also members of the Church, compared to 93 percent of the young people living in central Utah.

The youth living in the areas outside of Utah—the low and moderate religious ecologies—did report facing significantly more pressure from friends and acquaintances to participate in inappropriate behavior. For example, over 40 percent of the young men and young women living outside Utah experience pressure from friends to drink beer, wine, and liquor as compared to 25 percent of the youth living in Utah County. (Table 3.1 reports the percent of LDS teenagers who said they had been pressured by their friends to engage in the various delinquent

## Table 3.1
## Percent of LDS Youth Whose Friends Have Pressured Them to Commit Offenses Against Others, Against Property, and Status Offenses, by Religious Ecology and Gender

| | East Coast | | Pacific Northwest | | Utah Valley | |
|---|---|---|---|---|---|---|
| | Males (N=632) | Females (N=754) | Males (N=251) | Females (N=363) | Males (N=460) | Females (N=598) |
| **Offenses Against Others** | | | | | | |
| Cursed or swore at a parent | 16% | 20% | 16% | 17% | 12% | 13% |
| Pushed, shoved, or hit a parent | 7 | 7 | 6 | 4 | 5 | 5 |
| Made obscene phone calls | 32 | 36 | 47 | 42 | 36 | 30 |
| Purposely picked on kids/made fun of/called names | 69 | 64 | 73 | 60 | 59 | 48 |
| Physically beat up other kids | 40 | 16 | 46 | 12 | 34 | 10 |
| Took money or other things by using force or threats | 11 | 3 | 14 | 5 | 8 | 4 |
| Joined in a gang fight | 15 | 4 | 8 | 4 | 9 | 3 |
| **Offenses Against Property** | | | | | | |
| Took something from a store without paying for it | 50% | 30% | 47% | 26% | 36% | 12% |
| Stole anything more than $20 | 16 | 6 | 22 | 10 | 15 | 7 |
| Stole anything less than $20 | 49 | 27 | 49 | 27 | 38 | 20 |
| Took car or motor vehicle without owner's permission | 10 | 10 | 13 | 10 | 17 | 18 |
| Threw things at cars, people, or buildings | 56 | 26 | 53 | 29 | 52 | 27 |
| Broke into a building, car, house, etc. | 21 | 8 | 14 | 6 | 19 | 8 |
| Purposely ruined/damaged someone else's property or possessions | 47 | 27 | 53 | 28 | 41 | 25 |
| **Status Offenses** | | | | | | |
| Smoked cigarettes | 46% | 40% | 43% | 36% | 30% | 22% |
| Used "smokeless" or chewing tobacco | 29 | 7 | 36 | 16 | 18 | 6 |
| Drank alcoholic beverages (beer, wine, liquor) | 49 | 53 | 40 | 41 | 27 | 24 |
| Used marijuana ("grass," "pot") | 19 | 16 | 23 | 25 | 17 | 12 |
| Used cocaine ("crack," "coke") | 10 | 6 | 10 | 7 | 5 | 5 |
| Used other drugs (heroin, LSD, amphetamines, etc.) | 12 | 9 | 10 | 10 | 9 | 6 |
| Run away from home | 15 | 17 | 11 | 17 | 13 | 16 |
| Skipped school without a legitimate excuse | 58 | 62 | 61 | 72 | 68 | 61 |
| Cheated on a test | 76 | 77 | 72 | 75 | 67 | 68 |
| Read sexually explicit or pornographic books or magazines | 64 | 34 | 60 | 26 | 44 | 15 |
| Watched sexually explicit/pornographic movies, videos, or TV | 63 | 48 | 53 | 35 | 42 | 21 |
| Been involved in heavy petting | 35 | 45 | 28 | 39 | 20 | 25 |

behaviors.) Greater pressure is also evident for LDS youth outside of Utah to do drugs and to participate in premarital sexual activity. The differences in peer pressure are greater for Word of Wisdom and morality behavior since many religions, communities, and families accept and may even foster such behavior. Differences in pressure to commit actions that injure others or to steal or damage others' property appear, but are not as large. It was somewhat discouraging to discover that teens living in the "heart of Zion"—the high religious ecology of Utah County—experience significant pressure from friends who are members of the Church to deviate from the straight and narrow gospel path.

Table 3.2 reports the percent of youth with "most" or "all" of their friends participating in delinquent behaviors. An ecological or geographical difference is apparent in friends' examples, as those youth living in the mission field have many more friends who engage in delinquent activities. For example, "most or all" of the friends of over 40 percent of the youth living on the East Coast drink alcoholic beverages and most of the friends of 20 percent of teens in the Pacific Northwest drink as compared to only 7 percent of the friends of young people in Utah. As with peer pressure, the differences are greater for status offenses. Not surprisingly, more young men than young women reported their friends were delinquent.

The tables document in detail the oppressive pressure LDS teens experience from their friends to break the laws of the land and to violate Church standards. Although youth living in Utah don't experience as much peer pressure as youth living in the mission field, it is certainly a powerful negative influence because the pressure they face comes primarily from other members of the Church. In some respects this can be as hard, if not harder, to withstand than continual peer pressure from friends who do not have those religious values. Both groups of teens—Utah and the mission field—are exposed to rather strong influences from their friends to violate their personal standards. It was somewhat disconcerting to note that the young

## Table 3.2
## Percent of LDS Youth Whose Friends Have Committed Offenses Against Others, Against Property, and Status Offenses, by Religious Ecology and Gender

| | East Coast | | Pacific Northwest | | Utah Valley | |
| --- | --- | --- | --- | --- | --- | --- |
| | Males (N=632) | Females (N=754) | Males (N=261) | Females (N=370) | Males (N=460) | Females (N=598) |
| **Offenses Against Others** | | | | | | |
| Cursed or swore at one of parents | 19% | 31% | 11% | 16% | 8% | 9% |
| Pushed, shoved, or hit one of parents | 5 | 8 | 2 | 3 | 2 | 2 |
| Openly defied a teacher or official at school | 23 | 20 | 3 | 3 | 6 | 3 |
| Made obscene phone calls | 10 | 12 | 16 | 14 | 12 | 12 |
| Purposely picked on kids/made fun of/called names | 36 | 34 | 33 | 23 | 22 | 10 |
| Physically beat up other kids | 15 | 7 | 8 | 2 | 9 | 3 |
| Took money or other things by using force or threats | 3 | 2 | 2 | 1 | 1 | 0 |
| Joined in a gang fight | 4 | 2 | 1 | 2 | 2 | 2 |
| **Offenses Against Property** | | | | | | |
| Took something from a store without paying for it | 14% | 7% | 13% | 7% | 10% | 4% |
| Stole anything more than $20 | 2 | 1 | 3 | 1 | 3 | 2 |
| Stole anything less than $20 | 25 | 12 | 19 | 10 | 14 | 7 |
| Took car or motor vehicle without owner's permission | 4 | 2 | 1 | 2 | 4 | 5 |
| **Status Offenses** | | | | | | |
| Smoked cigarettes | 19% | 23% | 12% | 17% | 7% | 7% |
| Used "smokeless" or chewing tobacco | 9 | 4 | 6 | 6 | 3 | 2 |
| Drank alcoholic beverages (beer, wine, liquor) | 37 | 48 | 15 | 25 | 8 | 6 |
| Used marijuana ("grass," "pot") | 6 | 6 | 6 | 11 | 5 | 4 |
| Used cocaine ("crack," "coke") | 1 | 2 | 1 | 1 | 0 | 2 |
| Used other drugs (heroin, LSD, amphetamines, etc.) | 3 | 3 | 2 | 3 | 2 | 2 |
| Run away from home | 2 | 3 | 2 | 3 | 3 | 3 |
| Skipped school without a legitimate excuse | 40 | 41 | 37 | 43 | 40 | 36 |
| Cheated on a test | 38 | 40 | 30 | 35 | 27 | 24 |
| Read sexually explicit or pornographic books or magazines | 28 | 12 | 20 | 7 | 13 | 3 |
| Watched sexually explicit/pornographic movies, videos, or TV | 27 | 18 | 19 | 10 | 13 | 4 |
| Been involved in heavy petting | 29 | 38 | 15 | 26 | 9 | 10 |
| Had sexual intercourse | 20 | 22 | 6 | 12 | 3 | 3 |

women experience equal if not greater pressure to sin than do the young men for many of the delinquent activities.

The results of the test of the model, as seen in figure 3, confirmed that peer pressure is the most significant predictor of delinquency. The relationship is obvious: if a teen's friends encourage and perhaps challenge him or her to participate in delinquent activities, the youth generally goes along. Also, just having friends who do these things is an indirect enticement. Youth want to belong to a group, and they often feel that joining in inappropriate behaviors will establish their acceptance. Direct pressure is by far the strongest influence, but friends' example also makes an important contribution to understanding delinquency among LDS youth. Interestingly, youth outside the predominantly LDS areas of Utah experience greater peer pressure, yet they have about the same level of delinquency as youth in Utah. This suggests that either they are exposed to other influences that inhibit delinquency or else they compensate in some way to reduce the impact of the extra peer pressure.

Fortunately, all is not lost—parents can help their teenagers gain friends who will support them in keeping the commandments. In addition, parents can help their adolescent children resist the influence of friends and associates who pressure them to participate in delinquent activity.

## Figure 3.1
## The Relationship of Peer Influences to Delinquency

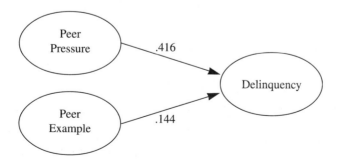

# Selecting Good Friends: Accentuating the Positive

Parents often feel helpless to influence the selection of those with whom their teenagers hang out. Indeed, establishing friendship ties is largely beyond parents' ability to control. Sometimes teens lack the ability or desire to seek out good friends. Other times, those good kids that parents desire their children to associate with refuse to accept them, and thus their children end up with less-than-desirable friends. Although parents are limited in choosing friends for their kids, they can influence the process.

## The Neighborhood

Long-range planning can surround your children with peers who may become the kind of friends you desire. Living in a neighborhood with a low rate of delinquency, infrequent gang activity, little drug use, and with schools having reputations for academic success increases association with children from good families who value education and are also desirous of their children maturing into competent adults. Young children play with those in the neighborhood; hopefully such friendships will persist in junior and senior high school. We are not suggesting that parents sell their homes and switch neighborhoods, but when moves do occur, children's friendship opportunities should be a major consideration.

## Family Friends

Another long-range suggestion is for parents to develop friendships with couples whose children will make good friends for their children. Families can invite other families to visit an amusement park, go on a camping trip, have a picnic, attend a sporting event, or enjoy some other fun activity with them. They can also invite the children from the other families to join their children in activities so they identify with the family. The stronger the ties between the two families, the more family members will be linked to each other. Even if the teenagers from the two families don't develop a close friendship, they will likely help each other out in the neighborhood and high school. They may speak up in each other's defense or give a "positive character reference" at a crucial time.

## Friendship Skills

As children work their way through elementary school and into junior high, it is important to teach them social skills that will help them make friends. Children should be taught to be considerate of others, to be a friend to those who are less popular, and to be more friendly and outgoing in general. Parents can encourage their children to be of service to other children, such as helping them with homework, teaching them sports skills, or helping them do their chores, all of which will certainly enhance their popularity. Finally parents can give their children experience in asking others to join them in an activity. *"It might have been helpful to have lessons about how to have friends when I was young,"* one young man reported when asked what his parents could have done to help him choose good friends. A teenager who develops such skills will have more potential friends from which to select his or her close sidekicks and will experience less rejection from peers.

## Participation in Activities

Probably the single most effective thing parents can do to help their teens select good friends is to encourage them to participate in groups, organizations, and activities that will involve them with other good kids. Several youth credited their extracurricular activities with linking them with supportive friends. For example one young woman said: *"I usually made friends with people who were in similar activities as me, like track and cross country. I also was in a few accelerated classes and got to know the kids in them who were pretty good kids and were committed to school."* A young man shared a similar experience: *"Most of my friends came from activities I was involved in, i.e., track, dance, and swim team."* One young man explained how to use an extracurricular activity to change peer groups: *"If you've messed up [have bad friends] and you need to start over with new friends, start a new extracurricular activity. You'll meet an entirely new group of people and have a fresh start. It may be a good idea to let your old friends know you're trying to do better. If they don't want to change too, it won't be hard to say good-bye."* A young woman credited her parents for their support, which took the form of paying extra fees, paying for music lessons, providing rides, and taking time away from home. *"My parents supported me in school and extracurricular activities that took up most of my time and kept me out of trouble. Also, I was with the best kids in these activities."*

There are many opportunities for young people to become involved in school activities, such as accelerated classes, athletic teams, band, drama, National Honor Society, choir, debate club, and many other kinds of productive and character-building activities.

Finally, community activities—including a local theater group or service club—offer the same opportunity for teenagers to associate with other teens of good reputation who share similar values and aspirations. As a general rule, youth involved in these kinds of activities are serious about school and don't have the time, energy, or inclination to engage in delinquent behaviors.

## *Church Friends*

A large number of youth who attended high school in the mission field areas of our study reported they found their friends at Church. *"The friends I chose to spend my free time with were those I knew from seminary and Church classes,"* noted one young man. Another indicated that his parents *"encouraged me to participate in seminary, Mutual activities, and other Church activities. These were the places where I found better friends."* Teenagers participating in Church activities often required considerable parental sacrifice to provide rides or to allow the youth to take the family car. In some cases the distances were considerable, but parents felt the friendship potential was worth the time and expense. In addition, parents can host activities for LDS youth. *"My parents were willing to help us gather LDS kids together,"* replied one young woman. She continued: *"Although it meant opening their home to a bunch of noisy teenagers, it gave us a place to be together and build friendships. My parents made sure I was able to attend all the Church events—even if it meant driving hours away to get to a youth dance. It meant we could build these relationships with other LDS kids."*

Some of the young people surveyed mentioned they had developed friendships with nonmembers in junior high and tried to maintain these during high school. Sometimes as they got older, their friends started participating in activities inappropriate for members of the Church, and the LDS youth felt estranged from them. One young woman reported that she eventually sought friends from Church because they had similar values: *"I grew up in California. Most of my friends were not LDS. My friends were great until our senior year. Then they all began partying and drinking. It was very hard not to join in. I just wouldn't go to the parties. This was the best way for me to keep away from the drinking and drugs. I eventually was not as close to these friends and developed much closer friendships with kids at Church."* A similar story was told by a young man: *"At first all my friends were nonmembers and had high standards. But as we got older, they started drinking and smoking and doing other things that I would not participate in. I then decided to be with other people with standards like me, members of the Church. This was difficult at first, but it is what I wanted to do. My old friends would still continue to bother me about going to their parties, but I just said 'no thanks.'"*

It is difficult, and probably painful, for LDS teenagers to see longtime friends start to engage in activities that are inappropriate for LDS youth. But as we stated in chapter 2, a sizable proportion of high school seniors across the country drink (80 percent), experiment with drugs (30 percent), and engage in premarital sex (70 percent). Some LDS youth try to maintain ties with wayward friends by avoiding weekend parties or being the "designated driver." Such tactics are temporary at best, and tempting at worst, as the LDS teens find themselves growing apart from those with whom they have less and less in common.

Latter-day Saint youth living in areas where there are relatively few members of the Church face the hard issue of whether to date those not of our faith. There is no doubt that many nonmember teens are good kids with high values and similar standards. There may be little risk in dating them, but there is still risk. On the other hand, many non-LDS teens have definitely different values. One young woman from our young adult study advised other LDS youth: *"Don't date nonmembers. Bottom line, it is just too hard—even the so-called 'nice guys.' 'Good' can never be a relative term; members of the Church hopefully realize the absolutes. Nonmembers have different and twisted versions of what is right and wrong."* We speculated in chapter 2 that more LDS young women than young men violate the law of chastity largely because they date older nonmembers who are sexually experienced. LDS young women are often not prepared to defend themselves against their wily, seductive tactics. Parents should counsel their teens to choose carefully whom they date, especially when considering dating nonmembers.

## *Welcome in Our Home*

Another good way for parents to help their teens develop friendships with good kids is to make their home available as a place to hang out. *"My parents always encouraged me to invite my friends over, which in turn encouraged me to have friends that I wasn't ashamed to have in our home"* was how a young man credited his parents with guiding him to associate with good friends. One young woman wished her parents had been more hospitable to her friends: *"I wish they would have encouraged me to have more activities at our house. The trials I faced always happened at someone else's home. I don't think my friends would have even considered doing certain things in our home."* It is interesting that she felt going to her friends' homes placed her in greater temptation than if she would have taken her friends home with her.

In addition to encouraging teenagers to host activities in their home, parents can increase the attraction by making their friends feel welcome. This not only strengthens friendships between the youth but also creates ties between parents and their kids' friends. Also, parents can make the family room available to impromptu as well as planned activities. We have discovered that earplugs allow us to get the sleep we need while our teenagers and their friends played games, watched sports on TV, viewed appropriate videos, or participated in other wholesome activities in the adjacent family room. Removal of an earplug would reaffirm that they were home participating in activities with friends we knew and approved of.

# Resisting Peer Pressure:
# Minimizing the Negative

In the beginning of this chapter we recounted the youths' reports of the endemic peer pressure they face in school and in the community. Even though a teenager's best friends may be good kids who support his or her righteousness, the youth is exposed to extensive pressure from other friends, associates, and acquaintances to participate in illegal and immoral activities. In a high school setting, LDS youth are thrown into contact not only with friends but also a wide variety of youth who invite and sometimes pressure them to do things against gospel standards. Generally the youth must make their stand against such pressures without close parental support. But parents are not helpless in this fight.

## *Make a Stand*

When we asked about how they had resisted peer pressures while in high school, college students overwhelmingly replied, "Make a clear statement of your values and then stick to them." One young woman explained it this way: *"I made sure all of my friends knew what I believed from day one. After that, if they asked me to do something against my beliefs I would just laugh. I would say, 'You know I don't do that, why are you even asking?'"* A similar sentiment was expressed by a young man: *"BE FIRM about what you believe. Never compromise! Because the first time you do you will lose the respect of your peers."* One young woman reported that once she had made her standards clear to her friends, they actually helped her to keep them. *"My friends all knew my standards and didn't invite me to participate in activities they knew I'd be uncomfortable with. In fact, they would warn me against things (movies or song lyrics) that they knew I would not be comfortable seeing."* The same experience was reported by another young woman: *"In Minnesota there are hardly any Mormons. Everyone knew who I was and they knew my standards. It was to the point where they wouldn't let me do bad things, even if I had wanted to."*

The implication from these comments is that parents should encourage their teenagers to share their personal behavioral standards with their friends during the initial stages of the friendship. This doesn't mean the LDS teen should get on a soapbox and loudly proclaim that he or she doesn't smoke, but rather that the teen take, or perhaps make, an opportunity to share his or her standards with friends. The trick is to look for a lead-in or an opening in a conversation to say "I am LDS, and as you probably know we don't drink or smoke." There seem to be two benefits from teens declaring personal standards to their friends. First, they experience considerably less pressure to violate standards of the Church since many, although not all, of their friends will refrain from exerting such pressure. Second, some of their friends become supporters who buffer the teen from pressures by other friends or associates.

## *Avoid Bad Situations*

The young adults we surveyed acknowledged that when they were in high school they had a pretty good idea of what went on at parties and other activities. Thus many of them stated that avoiding situations where immoral activities were going on was the key to not being pressured into participation. A young woman stated: *"Mostly, I just never placed myself anywhere there could be a problem with keeping my standards. If I ever found myself trapped, I just walked away without any lengthy discussion."* One young man bluntly said, *"Don't get yourself into bad situations."* These young adults remembered how strong the pressures to break the commandments can be in certain situations and found it was easier to avoid them. Thus, parents can discuss with their teens the dangerous places in their young lives and then encourage them to stay away.

Another young adult credited his parents with playing an active role in keeping him away from temptation: *"Sometimes my parents wouldn't allow me to go to certain activities because they knew the situations would bring me down. They made sure I knew that it wasn't because they didn't trust me. They just knew it was a place where the Spirit couldn't be."* Several of the young adults appreciated that their parents gave them the right to invoke parental disapproval as an excuse for refusing to do something against gospel standards. *"My father said if I was ever in a bad situation, I could use him as an excuse to get out of it,"* one young man confided. A young woman stated that she had her parents' permission to tell friends, *"My folks will kill me if I did that; I would be grounded forever."* This type of parental support appeared to give many youth an excuse that friends would accept and allowed the youth to avoid the temptation without losing face with peers.

## *Keep Talking*

Many young adults noted that being able to confide in parents and ask their advice was something that really helped them resist peer pressure. In a later chapter we will discuss in greater detail how to strengthen family connectedness. A young woman indicated that discussing peer pressure with her parents gave her the courage to resist: *"Sometimes it is easy to think that nothing is wrong when you are really slipping. Be very open with your parents. Even though you are doing things wrong, they will help you."* A young man repeated this counsel: *"My parents talked openly with me about what is right and wrong. In this way the temptations to do wrong were lessened."* One young woman identified youths' need for acceptance and appealed to parents to love and support their children so that they won't turn to others: *"Parents should be positive supports for their children or else they will go elsewhere looking for acceptance and the reinforcement that people like them. They get caught in the 'I will do anything to please you syndrome.'"* Dinner table conversations, heart-to-heart talks when youth come in at night, father-teen interviews, and talks with mother over cookies and root beer are golden opportunities for parents to fortify their teens' resolve to resist peer pressure. Parents can acknowledge the powerful forces of evil their teenagers face, provide suggestions, share their own experiences in meeting life's challenges, and offer emotional support.

## Parents Monitoring Peers

It was interesting that many of the LDS teens in high school wished their parents had been more strict with them, while only a few complained about too much parental control. A number of the young adults expressed a regret that their parents hadn't exerted more control over their hanging out with bad friends or their going to parties where they faced strong temptations. A young man's comment illustrates this sentiment: *"I almost wish that my parents had trusted me less. They never worried about my standards so we never discussed them. I was very tempted to do things that were wrong, and sometimes I gave in. But I never felt I could tell my parents."* A young woman reported similar feelings: *"Sometimes I wish my parents would have been a little more strict and kept me on a tighter leash. I found too many easy opportunities to be deceptive and do bad things without their knowing. I had to try hard to be honest with them."*

Others indicated that their parents' monitoring of their activities really helped them avoid or resist peer pressures. *"It might sound kind of controlling, but my parents 'monitored' who I spent time with,"* one young women revealed. She continued, *"They knew all my friends that I hung out with and they knew their parents. They took the time to develop some sort of relationship with my friends, even if it was just briefly talking to them."* A young man echoed the value of parental monitoring: *"They set limits for me, curfews; they always wanted to know where I was and when I would be home. I also got grounded or had privileges taken away if I acted like an idiot."* Another teen reported, *"My parents give me extra privileges when I am with friends they approve of."*

Parents can help their teenagers avoid peer pressures to sin by monitoring and using their influence to keep them away from situations where inappropriate activities are likely to occur. Parents also can assist by using their influence to encourage their teenage children to associate with good kids of whom they approve. These monitoring activities take considerable courage, emotional effort, and time on the parents' part, but yield substantial dividends. In chapter 5 we discuss this kind of parental monitoring in greater detail and offer a number of specific suggestions for accomplishing it.

## *Strengthen Commitment to Gospel Principles*

Even though parents are not physically present with their teenagers when they are in school or out with friends, their influence can be with them. The family and activities in the home can fortify teens to resist the pressure encountered in the wicked world. One young man lamented, *"I wish my parents would have had more family activities like prayer together, meals together, family home evening, etc. If I could have seen the importance of family on earth, it would have aided me in dealing with my friends."* The prophets and other Church leaders have repeatedly counseled parents to spiritually strengthen their children through family activities in the home. The family can help children internalize gospel principles, which is directly linked to a youth's ability to resist peer pressure and is so vital in assisting teenagers to become righteous adults. In chapter 4 we will discuss the role of religion and how parents can help their children internalize the gospel.

Research has clearly demonstrated over and over again that peer influence is the most powerful force in deciding whether a teenager becomes involved in delinquency. This is also true of LDS youth, who often find themselves experiencing considerable pressure to disobey gospel principles. The pressure is almost overwhelming to violate their unique Word of Wisdom and chastity standards. Fortunately, parents can assist their teenage children to choose good friends to hang out with who will at least not tear them down and perhaps will actually build them up. Within the walls and halls of the junior and senior high schools, LDS youth face an array of peers who expose them to the full range of wickedness running rampant in society. One of the greatest challenges facing parents is to fortify their children in their struggles to live righteously in the face of such pressures.

# 4

# PUTTING ON THE ARMOR OF GOD

## THE POWER OF PERSONAL SPIRITUALITY

The Apostle Paul in the New Testament and the Lord himself in modern revelation declared that in order to "be able to withstand the evil day" one must be clothed in the "armor of God" (see Ephesians 6:11–18; also D&C 27:15–18). This protective armor consists of such things as truth, righteousness, the gospel, faith, salvation, and the Spirit of the Lord. The scriptures attest that true religiosity will indeed insulate people from the "fiery darts of the wicked." While many social scientists scoff at the power of religion to affect behavior and deter delinquency, the results of our study (as well as common sense) confirm what the scriptures teach about the protective power of the "armor of God." Many of the youth's comments illustrate how their religious values and faith help them to counteract peer pressure and overcome the significant spiritual challenges they face in their lives:

*I love being a member of the Church. I have developed a personal testimony of the gospel. I know that I am a daughter of God and that belief helps me resist temptation.*

*Because of the training I have received in the Church and my own personal study of the scriptures and personal prayer, I have the guidance of the Spirit, which I associate with my conscience. This has been the leading force in encouraging me and strengthening my desires to do what is right and true. This internal motivation has been the most powerful influence in my life in helping me to live the standards of the Church.*

*My parents and Church leaders have been a good influence. I am very grateful for their strength and belief in the gospel. I believe because of these people, the scriptures, and my own belief in Heavenly Father and Jesus Christ that I am not personally affected by the negative things I face. I have no desire to do things or participate in things that would bring me shame or damage my spirit.*

Perhaps one of the most important findings of this study was that religion in and of itself—not just living in a religious ecology such as a predominantly LDS community—does indeed have a significant effect on the behavior of Latter-day Saint teenagers. Religious values, beliefs, and experiences are clearly and directly related to avoiding inappropriate and immoral behaviors.

Examining the religious beliefs and practices of the LDS youth in our study yielded some interesting insights. As with the results of the levels of LDS teen delinquency, there again was great news, good news, and not-so-good news. As can be seen in table 4.1, the LDS youth in our study are generally a highly religious group, regardless of where they live. Over 95 percent of these young men and women reported that they believe that God lives, that Jesus is the Christ, and that Joseph Smith was indeed a true prophet of God. Approximately 90 percent of the youth reported that they plan to marry in the temple and remain active in the Church. Over 80 percent reported that their relationship with God was "very important" to them. These remarkably high levels of religious belief demonstrate the great news.

# Table 4.1

## Personal Religious Beliefs and Practices of LDS Youth, by Region

| | East Coast Agree | Pacific Northwest Agree | Utah Valley Agree |
|---|---|---|---|
| **Religious Beliefs** | | | |
| God lives and is real | 96% | 96% | 95% |
| Jesus Christ is divine son of God | 97 | 98 | 97 |
| God really does answer prayers | 88 | 90 | 89 |
| Joseph Smith saw God and Christ | 92 | 95 | 96 |
| The President of the Church is a prophet | 94 | 96 | 96 |
| Book of Mormon is true | 93 | 95 | 94 |
| Church is guided by revelation | 92 | 95 | 94 |
| I plan to marry in the temple | 88 | 90 | 92 |
| **Public Behavior** | | | |
| Attend priesthood or Young Women | 83 | 81 | 74 |
| Attend sacrament meeting | 86 | 86 | 79 |
| Attend Sunday School | 84 | 81 | 69 |
| Attend social activities | 54 | 44 | 36 |
| Give testimony in meeting | 7 | 7 | 5 |
| **Private Behavior** | | | |
| Fast once each month | 34 | 37 | 43 |
| Pay full tithing | 55 | 57 | 56 |
| Read scriptures | 26 | 37 | 36 |
| Pray | 41 | 51 | 59 |
| **Spiritual Experiences** | | | |
| I have been guided by the Spirit with some of my problems or decisions | 75 | 84 | 87 |
| There have been times I felt the Holy Ghost | 81 | 85 | 86 |
| I have felt repentance and forgiveness | 67 | 63 | 70 |
| **Acceptance in Church** | | | |
| I sometimes feel like an outsider in the ward | 30 | 25 | 26 |
| I am well liked by members of my ward | 75 | 78 | 68 |
| I seem to fit in very well with the people in my ward | 63 | 65 | 61 |

When it came to public religious behavior, the teens showed quite high activity rates, with about 80 percent reporting that they regularly attended sacrament meetings, Sunday School, and priesthood or Young Women meetings. It is interesting to note, however, that the youth in the highest religious ecology—Utah County—actually had the lowest attendance percentages. Nevertheless, this evidence of high involvement in Church meetings and activities is very good news. Similarly, between 75 and 80 percent of the youth reported that they had a testimony of the gospel, felt the Spirit in their lives at times, and had earnestly tried to live the standards of the gospel throughout the past year. This also is good news!

The not-so-good news is found in the considerably lower levels of personal religious involvement. In contrast to the very high levels of public religious belief and activity, the individual involvement in vital private religious behaviors such as personal prayer, personal scripture study, fasting, and paying tithing is considerably lower. It is interesting to note the decline in the youth's levels of religiosity as the measurement moves from mere belief to personal practice. The highest percentages are in the areas of professed beliefs, which take little commitment or sacrifice. Next, comes the public behaviors. They are lower, but still relatively high. It requires effort to attend meetings, but there is also a more public expectation and pressure, such as parents or friends going to church with them. The lowest levels of religious practices are those that are just between the youth and the Lord. This is where real religious commitment is manifest, where there is no outward pressure or extrinsic reward. The actions come from within the heart and soul of the individual teen. It is not-so-good news to see that only half of these "highly religious" teenagers regularly pray privately and that only a third of them regularly read the scriptures on their own or fast each month. What makes these findings somewhat troubling is the fact that our results further showed that these private religious behaviors are the most important factors in helping youth resist peer pressures and temptations.

The religiosity of LDS teenagers seems to be virtually unaffected by where the youth live. It seems to make no difference whether a teenager lives in the heart of Utah, where there are many well-established wards and stakes, or whether they live in outlying areas with fewer members of the Church, or even in small branches. Generally speaking, LDS teens wherever they live believe in the gospel, have the beginnings of personal testimony, attend their meetings fairly regularly, and are at least trying to live Church standards. This too should be viewed as good news!

As previously noted, the religiosity of the LDS teens in our study proved to have a significant effect on their behavior. Religion was as powerful a deterrent of the delinquency among the youth living in minority Mormon areas like the East Coast and the Pacific Northwest as it was for the youth in the almost exclusively LDS communities of Utah County. In the diagram shown in figure 4.1, the strong relationship between the religious values of the LDS youth and their levels of delinquency is evidenced. The results (beta=-.191) would indicate that the stronger a youth is in the faith, the less likely he or she is to engage in inappropriate or immoral activities. While this comes as a "no brainer" to us, it goes against the grain of much of social science theory. It only makes sense that those youth (as well as adults) who have made religion an important part of their life and have experienced, to some degree at least, the "fruits" of their beliefs are better equipped to resist peer pressure and avoid delinquency and are less likely to choose delinquent friends.

# How Does Religion Make a Difference?

If someone were to ask us, "Does religion significantly affect the behavior of youth?" our answer would have to be: "Well, it depends

## Figure 4.1
## Relationship of Religiosity to Delinquency

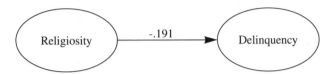

on what you mean by religion." One of the most important things we discovered in our studies was the identification of specific aspects of religion that appear to make the biggest difference in the lives of the young people. Not surprisingly, we found that some aspects of what one might characterize as being religious don't seem to affect behavior nearly as powerfully as other things do. For example, we examined five different dimensions of religiosity—religious beliefs, public religious behavior, private religious behavior, spiritual experiences, and acceptance in Church (social acceptance). We did additional statistical tests to determine the relative strength of each of these factors. Because religious beliefs, private religious behavior, and spiritual experiences were so closely related, they were combined into one dimension of religiosity we called spirituality. These three aspects of religiosity are the stuff of which a testimony of the gospel and commitment to the Church are made.

The results of these statistical tests are seen in figure 4.2. As can be seen, spirituality—as evidenced by the private religious behaviors and the degree to which the youth had experienced and internalized the gospel into their lives—was by far the strongest predictor of avoiding delinquent behavior in LDS youth as indicated by the -.333 beta coefficient. In other words, those youth for whom religion was an important internal aspect of their lives resisted peer pressure and avoided delinquency to a far greater extent than those youth who had not internalized gospel teachings. More important than attendance at meetings, the more young people engaged in such private acts of

## Figure 4.2
## Specific Aspects of Religiosity Predicting Delinquency

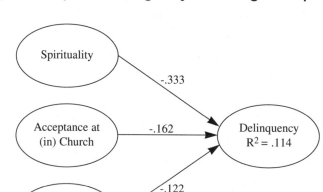

faith as personal prayer, fasting, and scripture study, the lower their levels of unrighteous behaviors.

The next most important aspect of religion that seems to prevent delinquency was the feelings of social acceptance in the ward, especially among other LDS young women and men. The more the youth felt truly loved and accepted by their church leaders and advisers and the more they were made to feel a part of their respective quorums and classes, the less likely they were to engage in the wrong kind of behaviors (beta= -.162).

Meanwhile, some of the factors that Church members have traditionally viewed as being important to the prevention of teen delinquency were not nearly as strong as these other aspects of religion. For example, public religious behavior, such as attendance at church meetings, showed a weak yet statistically significant relationship to delinquency (beta= -.122). Family religious practices such as family prayer, scripture study, and family home evening were not significantly related to lower levels of delinquency or immorality among

Latter-day Saint teenagers. These family activities and attendance at church meetings, as important as they are to the internalization of religious values, apparently do not in and of themselves counteract peer pressures to engage in unworthy behavior. Rather, it would seem that these activities promote strength to resist temptation to the degree to which they encourage the youth to pray, fast, read the scriptures, and have their own personal, spiritual experiences. In comparing these three important aspects of religiosity—public religious behavior, acceptance in Church, and spirituality—it appears that *the key to deterring delinquency is not found merely in getting the youth into the Church, but rather in getting the gospel and personal testimony into the youth.*

The results of this study empirically validate the teachings the prophets of God have given to the Church for generations. When we see the power that personal spirituality can have in the lives of the youth, we can better understand why latter-day prophets and apostles consistently counsel parents, Church leaders, teachers, and youth advisers to increase their efforts in helping youth more fully experience the gospel and more fully inwardly feel its spiritual benefits in their lives. "You are not merely to teach lessons, or expound doctrines, or set up tools, and prescribe programs," President Spencer W. Kimball counselled. "Your success is not only setting up ideals, but in *motivating [the youth] to put these ideals into their lives.*" (Spencer W. Kimball, "Circles of Exaltation," in *Charge to Religious Educators,* 2nd edition [Salt Lake City: The Church of Jesus Christ of Latter-day Saints, 1981], p. 20; italics added.) Not only the statistical results of the study but also hundreds of comments by the youth themselves confirm what President James E. Faust declared:

> Generally, those children who make the decision to abstain from drugs, alcohol, and illicit sex, are those who have adopted and internalized the strong values of their homes as lived by their par-

ents. In times of difficult decisions they are most likely to follow the teachings of their parents rather than the examples of their peers or the sophistries of the media which glamorize alcohol consumption, illicit sex, infidelity, dishonesty, and other vices. . . .

What seems to cement parental [and Church] teachings and values in place in children's lives is a firm belief in deity. When this belief becomes part of their very souls, they have inner strength. (In Conference Report, October 1990, pp. 42–43.)

The comments from the teenagers themselves support Elder Faust's observation:

*The most important influence that has helped me through the negative peer pressures and temptations I have faced is the knowledge I received through my own testimony of the gospel that I could turn to my Heavenly Father for purpose and direction. In junior high I prayed diligently and sincerely for a good group of friends. Answers and direction came that I knew were not my own. My testimony brought a peace that sustained me during those difficult times.*

*The strongest pressure to live the standards of the Church has come from my own conscience. Personal study of the scriptures, personal prayer, the guidance of the Spirit—which I often associate with my conscience—have been the leading force in encouraging me and strengthening my desires to do what is right and true. This internal motivation has been the most powerful of all pressures!*

*I realize that all I need is faith and if I'm worried I can pray to the Lord for guidance. I am really grateful to be a member of the Church. I don't even think of being a member of the Church as a pressure. I think of it as a privilege. I wouldn't want to be anything else out in the world today.*

*Some of the strength to avoid temptation has come to me from scripture reading, writing in my journal, personal prayer, attending general conference, and reading current Church writings, as well as going to the temple to do baptisms for the dead on a regular basis.*

*Because my parents are kind of wishy-washy, I have strived to gain a firm testimony of the gospel for myself. I have a lot of family problems, as lots of teenagers tend to, but my testimony—that I gained independently—has helped me be strong.*

*The strongest pressures to live the gospel come from deep within myself as I learn more about the Savior and what He did for me. I love Christ so much and am thankful for the gift of the Atonement.*

A theme that seems to be woven throughout each of these statements is that the gospel has power to help teenagers (as well as the rest of us) resist temptation and strengthen them against peer pressure only when it comes from within their own hearts and souls. Such protective power doesn't come merely from outward evidence of religiosity, such as attendance and active involvement in church programs and activities, but flows from inward spirituality and personal testimony. We need to narrow the gap between the *external* (professed beliefs and Church attendance) and the *internal* (the spirituality that guides behavior and gives strength to resist temptation).

As priesthood leaders we saw the problems in the lives of youth when the internal spirituality was significantly lower than their external religious activity. A most revealing example of that is the case of a young woman who became pregnant at the age of fifteen but insisted that she would "never disobey the prophet's counsel not to date before sixteen!" Espousing an external religious belief—for example, that we are led by living prophets—or even holding to a rigid external religious standard—like not dating before age sixteen—without a corresponding internalization of the principles associated with those beliefs and standards does not necessarily affect behavior. On the other hand, personal spirituality and internalization of the gospel leads to personal commitment, which always affects behavior! Being clothed with the "armor of God" that can "quench the fiery darts of the wicked" requires an internalization of gospel principles. For religion to have that kind of power in the lives of youth, it must be more than just something they *do,* it must be something they *are.*

## What Parents Can Do to Help Youth Internalize Gospel Principles

Youth are not left completely on their own to make the gospel an integral part of their personal lives. While each must plant the seed himself, a fertile seedbed and a nurturing environment is gained through a spiritually supportive family. Parents can do much to help youth internalize gospel principles and develop a solid spiritual foundation. "The home and family have vital roles in cultivating and developing personal faith and testimony," Elder M. Russell Ballard of the Quorum of the Twelve Apostles declared. "The family is the basic unit of society; the best place for individuals to build faith and strong testimonies is in righteous homes filled with love. . . . Strong faithful families have the best opportunity to produce strong, faithful members of the Church." (In Conference Report, Apr. 1996, p. 112.)

Elder Joe J. Christensen of the Presidency of the Quorum of the Seventy likewise gave a specific charge to parents to "create a spiritual environment" in which children can have their own spiritual experiences and to "help them build their own personal testimonies."

> We parents need to take seriously our responsibility to provide religious training in the home so that our children will in turn take religion seriously and personally. . . .
>
> One of the most effective ways to gain personal spiritual experiences and testimony is to become personally involved in serving, searching, pondering, and praying. . . .

Praying, holding family home evenings, and studying the scriptures with our children are important foundations. As we strive to create a spiritual environment, our family members can be led to those experiences that will help them build their own personal testimonies. (*One Step at a Time* [Salt Lake City: Deseret Book Co., 1996], pp. 90–92.)

From the results of our study, several important suggestions emerged as to how parents can specifically help their children make the gospel an important part of their lives.

## Be a Good Example

Someone once wisely observed, "Children seldom hear their parents, but they always emulate them." The righteous example of parents who have made the gospel the very core of their souls provides youth with a living, breathing object lesson of what true religiosity is all about. Many of the teenagers in our studies identified the personal examples of their parents as the most important influence in their lives in leading them to internalize the gospel.

*My parents' examples in living the teachings of Christ helped me internalize the gospel's principles in my life. Although this may not be very specific, the most important thing was just seeing in them that the gospel and Church were central to their lives. It was evident in every aspect of their lives.*

*The most influential person in my life is my mother. Her example of perfect faith and righteousness instilled in me a desire to be righteous too. Her example helped me to get through some tough times in my own life.*

*My parents always set the example of going to church and hold-*

*ing family prayer and home evening. But more than that I was impressed by their examples on a personal level. They never swore, no R-rated movies, their service to others, and most important was their total honesty, regardless of the situation. They really live the gospel!*

The old adage, "I cannot hear what you are saying because your actions speak louder than your words," is certainly true within the walls of a home. Nothing will turn off teenagers to the gospel more than to see their parents not practicing what they preach. This doesn't mean that we as parents have to be perfect, for that we certainly aren't and our children are quick to point out that fact. The youth are smart enough to know that we all have weaknesses, and at times we may not be as good as we ourselves desire. The damage is done, however, when parents go against the very teachings and standards they expect their children to espouse or try to pretend they are something they are not. It seems that teenagers have a special radar system in their spirits that can detect not only hypocrisy in parents but also insincerity. While it is true that many, if not most, teens won't even notice the clutter and chaos in their own bedrooms or notice the lateness of the hour when they are having fun, they are quick to observe parental hypocrisy and attempts to live a double standard. There can be no double standards in the home!

If we want our children to have testimonies of the gospel, to internalize its principles into their own lives, and to live by high standards of purity and integrity, we must do the same. You can't give what you don't have. "Our families can be given a gift to know what God would have them do and to learn it in a way that will encourage them to do it," declared Elder Henry B. Eyring of the Quorum of the Twelve. "God has provided such a guide. It is the Holy Ghost. We cannot give that to our family members as a companion, but they can earn it."

What we can do to create and transmit that legacy comes from an understanding of how testimony is instilled in our hearts. Since it is the Holy Ghost who testifies of sacred truth, we can do at least three things to make that experience more likely for our families. First, we can teach some sacred truth. Then we can testify that we know what we have taught is true. And then we must act so that those who hear our testimony see that our actions conform with what we said was true. The Holy Ghost will then confirm to them the truth of what we said and that we knew it to be true. . . .

We must find other ways to convey our legacy of testimony, but the process of teaching, testifying, and living the truth will be the same.

The scriptures, living prophets, and common sense tell us where to begin. We need to start with ourselves as parents. No program we follow or family tradition we create can transmit a legacy of testimony we do not have. (In Conference Report, Apr. 1996, pp. 84–85.)

## Hold Regular Family Prayer, Family Home Evening, and Family Scripture Study

Even though the statistical results of our study showed no significant relationship between these family religious practices and delinquency, that doesn't tell the whole story. Personal spirituality and religious conviction are directly linked to lower levels of delinquency. Family practices that promote religious internalization, such as family prayer, home evenings, and scripture study, do indeed affect adolescent behavior. There is a spiritual power in these family religious practices. We are to do these things in our homes not because we have to or merely to go through the motions but rather because the gospel is the center of our lives and these are manifestations of our love for not only the Lord but also our families. Our children, particularly teenagers, know when we are doing things just to be doing them as opposed to doing things that will bring us closer to the Lord and to each other. There isn't much saving power if we bring the family together for a home evening to pound a lesson into their heads "come hell or high water" and make our family miserable with contention, anger, or intimidation. Perhaps every parent feels frustrated at times in trying to faithfully hold family prayer, scripture study, and weekly home evenings when the children are restless and nothing seems to be "sinking in."

The young people in our study made many comments that should be encouraging to parents. They readily admit that there is a more powerful influence in these practices than what may appear on the surface. These hindsight comments from the young adults we interviewed show the lasting influence of family religious practices.

*I know I was a pain in the neck to my parents when it came to family prayer and family home evening. But I am thankful now that they didn't give up. It had more influence upon me than I was willing to admit at the time.*

*I pretended not to be listening when we had scripture study or lessons during family night, but more sank in than my parents thought.*

*My father loves to discuss doctrine, so when we would have FHE he would teach us important principles. We had great discussions and could feel the Spirit.*

*Even though my dad was inactive, he was always the one saying, "Time for family scripture reading" or "Prayer time." That showed me that he still wanted what was best for his family. It really helped our family.*

*Our family ate breakfast together, and Dad would read from the scriptures while the rest of us finished eating. He would teach us as he read. It was almost like having a daily family home evening.*

*My family always has scripture reading every day. It might seem like a pain, but by doing it it brings the Spirit into our home daily. When that happens you can't help but gain a stronger testimony.*

When we asked the young adults what they wished their parents would have done or done better to help their children better internalize gospel principles, many spoke of the need for more diligence in attending to family prayer, scripture study, and family home evening.

*I wish my parents would have had regular family home evening, family prayer, and scripture reading. I knew the gospel was important to them, but as converts they never grew up with such regular practices and so we didn't have it much in our home.*

*I wish my parents would have taught gospel principles more in our home, and I wish we would have read the scriptures as a family. That would have helped me a lot as I was growing up.*

*I wish that we would have had regular family home evening and family prayer. We did it once in a while, but I wish it had been more regular. I probably would have hated it at the time, but now I can see its importance.*

*I wish we would have had scripture study and FHE. To see my parents reading from the scriptures and teaching us from them would have really been helpful.*

The prophets of God have continually promised us that there would be not only an increase in gospel understanding and testimony when we faithfully and lovingly attend to these family practices but also that love, harmony, and closeness within the family would also increase. When the family home evening program was first introduced to the Church in 1915, the First Presidency promised the Saints "great blessings" if they would diligently seek to "gather their boys and girls about them in the home and teach them the word of the Lord." Undoubtedly, these promises apply also to family prayer and scripture study:

> If the Saints obey this counsel, we promise that great blessings will result. Love at home and obedience to parents will increase. Faith will be developed in the hearts of the youth of Israel, and they will gain power to combat the evil influences and temptations which beset them. (*Improvement Era,* June 1915, pp. 733–34.)

## *Teach Practical Applications of Gospel Principles*

The Lord has commanded parents to teach their children the doctrines of the gospel and "to pray, and to walk uprightly before the Lord" (see D&C 68:25–28). There seem to be two aspects of this sacred parental duty—first, to teach the doctrines of the kingdom, and second, to teach the children how to apply those doctrines to their daily lives. Many of the young adults in our study commented on this need for better parental instruction of their families in both doctrine and application:

> *I think parents in general don't teach the fundamental doctrines of the gospel nearly enough—things like faith, repentance, and the Atonement and how these things can be applied in daily life. Parents sometimes teach doctrines and principles, but don't talk specifically about the* why *and the* how. *As a result many teens know the teachings of the Church, but don't have a real testimony of the gospel's truth and of the Savior.*

Nephi spoke of "likening the scriptures" to ourselves (see 1 Nephi 19:23). This also applies in gospel teaching in our homes. Parents can do this by talking with their children about how the gospel can actually help us in our lives and apply it to dealing with specific temptations. Instead of our "likening the scriptures" to the lives of our teens, we can ask questions of them as to how they would apply or liken the gospel to their own unique challenges. This practical application of the gospel can be a two-way street—we can share with our families how the gospel applies to us and learn from them how they do the same.

One young woman in our study reported that her father would often talk to the kids about challenges or problems he was having at work. "How would you handle this?" he would ask his family. Pretty soon a good discussion would ensue, focusing on how gospel principles could solve life's real problems. The young lady observed, *"Now I realize he was helping us to see how the teachings of the gospel can actually work in life, rather than asking us to solve his problems."* Youth are much more likely to live the standards of the Church when they know not only the doctrines but also why they are to do what they are commanded, and what will be the practical benefits, right here and now, of living the gospel.

## Provide Opportunities for Spiritual Experiences

The cement that holds gospel teachings in place is personal spiritual experience. As was seen in the results cited previously, the most powerful effect of religiosity on behavior was personal spirituality—feeling the Spirit in one's own life and experiencing the fruits of gospel living. While real spiritual experiences cannot be manufactured or contrived, parents can provide opportunities and settings in which the teen may more easily feel close to the Lord. In this way, youth cannot only learn about the gospel and see it in action, but even more important they can *experience* it. Many of the young people talked about those special moments—many of which were spontaneous and unexpected—when they felt an outpouring of the Spirit.

> *Our family often did service for other people. This helped me to internalize the gospel because I could see the good we were doing for others and I realized how blessed we really were.*

> *Sunday dinner was always eaten together and at the table we each talked about what we had learned in church. Mom and Dad would also share what they had learned and would bear their testimony and share their feelings. This may seem too simple, but it really had an influence on me.*

> *Every fast Sunday we bear our testimonies to each other before we break our fast. One of the best spiritual experiences has been just singing hymns together at the piano.*

The Church organization—classes and quorums—can provide many opportunities to learn, serve, and feel the Spirit. There is an even greater spiritual impact, however, when these opportunities come from within the family. Many examples were given of family outings to the temple to do baptisms for the dead, family service projects, and impromptu testimony meetings that provided unique opportunities to feel things of the Spirit. Special occasions such as father's blessings, baptisms, or ordinations of family members also afforded opportunities for the entire family to see the gospel in action and to share feelings of love and testimony.

## Discuss and Share Feelings about the Gospel at Times Other Than Sunday

Parents can show their teenagers that the gospel is important in all aspects of their lives by sharing spiritual feelings, talking about gospel messages, and expressing gratitude at times other than just on Sunday or in formal religious settings. As one young lady in the study reported, *"As my dad washed the dishes in the sink or worked outside in the yard, sometimes out of the blue he would say, 'Heavenly Father, thank you for this beautiful day,' or 'Thank you, Father, for my daughter Amy.' This impressed me, and it taught me that I can approach the Lord and have spiritual feelings at any time in any setting."*

A major challenge youth have to overcome in order to have the strength to resist temptation is the tendency to view religion as merely "a church thing" or something that is done only on Sundays. This compartmentalization prevents them from seeing how the teachings of the gospel affect everyday lives and everyday situations. Seeing how the gospel is fully integrated into their parents' lives will help children understand how it can permeate every part of their own lives. As one teenage girl described:

*There are two specific places above the rest that I hold dear to my heart and see as great gospel learning places. This may sound strange, but they are my parents' king-size bed and the kitchen table. We almost always ate dinner together and there we would talk about our daily activities, but there was much more than that. We often would get into in-depth gospel discussions or talk about how we felt about something. Just these little things taught me so much. As for the bed—it had to be a king-size so all six of us kids could fit on it. This was a place where we could talk with Mom and Dad. I received so much comfort, guidance, and spiritual teaching there. These informal chats actually meant more to me than even family home evening lessons.*

## *Encourage Youth to Pray and Read Scriptures Privately*

One of the most important insights we gained is the need for teens to pray and study their scriptures on their own. We were quite surprised to discover that many of the teenagers felt no need to say their own personal prayers or read the scriptures by themselves, because they felt that it was enough that they were doing it with their families. Teenagers who pray and read scriptures not only with their families but also on their own will have greater spiritual strength than those who do not. It is important for families to do these things, but in order for youth to truly internalize the gospel they must pray and study individually in the quiet and privacy of their own space. Family prayer and scripture study, as important as they are, are more *external* activities, whereas personal prayer and scripture study become more *internal*.

The youth in our study who exercised faith in the Lord by consistently and conscientiously communing with their Heavenly Father in personal prayer showed greater strength to resist many of the peer pressures and temptations of the world. Similarly, those teens who also personally studied the scriptures on a regular, if not daily, basis evidenced significantly lower levels of unworthy behavior. These results empirically confirm the prophetic promises of latter-day seers such as President Ezra Taft Benson. "If you will earnestly seek guidance from your Heavenly Father, morning and evening," he promised the youth of the Church, "you will be given the strength to shun any temptation" ("A Message to the Rising Generation," *Ensign,* Nov. 1977, p. 32). President Benson also taught the youth (and the entire Church) of the personal power that comes from daily drinking from the fountain of truth found in the scriptures—particularly the Book of Mormon. As the Apostle Paul taught young Timothy, the scriptures have purpose and value beyond their use "for doctrine, for reproof, for correction, for instruction in righteousness." Studying the scriptures gives spiritual powers to the soul, "which are able to make thee wise unto salvation through faith which is in Christ Jesus" (see 2 Timothy 3:15–17). Again, as President Benson taught,

> it is not just that the Book of Mormon teaches us truth, though it indeed does that. It is not just that the Book of Mormon bears testimony of Christ, though it indeed does that too. But there is something more. There is a power in the book which will begin to flow into your lives the moment you begin a serious study of the book. *You will find greater power to resist temptation. You will find the power to avoid deception.* (*The Teachings of Ezra Taft Benson,* p. 54; italics added.)

We, as parents, need not try to solve all of our children's problems or answer all of their questions. "Have ye inquired of the Lord?" Nephi asked his brethren when they were doubting and questioning (see 1 Nephi 15:7–11). A more protective power will develop in the lives of youth if they learn to go to their Heavenly Father with their concerns and questions in personal prayer. It will mean more to them to find answers to gospel questions and life's difficult dilemmas through their own searching of the scriptures than just from parental preaching. We can teach them skills—we can direct them and guide them to the source, but the source must be the words of the Lord. As Alma learned, the word of God—obtained through prayer and scripture study—has a more powerful effect on the human soul than the sword or anything else. For this reason, parents should encourage their children to personally and individually "try the virtue of the word of God" (see Alma 31:5). This spiritual strength and personal power is evidenced in the insightful observations of the youth themselves.

*I am so blessed now because my parents encouraged me to pray and read the scriptures on my own.*

*I wish I would have prayed more and read my scriptures more. The times in my life when I have been the most unhappy were when I was not doing those things. I was too tired or just too lazy, but I was also unhappy. My problems seemed magnified when I didn't. I always keep that in mind now when I don't feel like praying or reading the scriptures.*

*My dad always reminds me, "Say your prayers." This reminds me that it is not enough to have family prayer. I must pray on my own.*

*My parents taught me how important personal revelation is and how I could find answers in the scriptures and receive answers to my prayers.*

*My parents encourage me to have faith and pray on my own so that I can have spiritual experiences for myself.*

*It was my parents' example that had the most effect on me. They always trusted me to make my own decisions. They would give thoughts and advice, but they left it up to me. But they would always counsel me to turn to the Lord and find out His will. In doing this it helped me to start to have spiritual experiences in my own life.*

Perhaps the capstone statement that summarizes this principle the best came from a response by a teenager to the question "What is the thing that helps you the most to live the gospel and resist temptation?" She said an awful lot in very few words: *"Reading the scriptures and prayer are things not to be done without!"*

## *Face the "Hard Questions"*

Sometimes our teens ask hard questions that may on the surface seem to indicate they doubt or challenge the Church. Do not dismiss our youth and think they have been brainwashed by anti-Mormons or are on the high road to apostasy. If we won't freak out, this can become a teaching opportunity and a chance to listen to the concerns, questions, and even doubts of our teen. If we don't know the answer, admit it and promise them to find out. It can become an opportunity for parent and child to study and talk and pray together. When we can demonstrate to the youth that the gospel holds up well under serious scrutiny, it strengthens their faith and confidence that the gospel has answers. In fact, the more seriously and conscientiously we seek to find answers in the scriptures and teachings of the Church, the more convinced we become of the truthfulness of the gospel. Since the gospel is indeed true, we need not be afraid to seek for honest, fair, and inspired answers to even the tough issues.

## *Encourage Youth to Attend Seminary*

Scores of teens identified seminary as the most important influence in their lives in helping them gain testimonies and have the strength to resist temptation. Sometimes teens won't listen to their parents preach but will receive the same gospel lessons delivered by someone they greatly respect and think is cool. As one of the teens stated: *"I love seminary. It makes me want to be good, and Brother _____ is a cool teacher!"*

> *My strongest help has been seminary. It has taught me a lot of what I hadn't known before. Now I do and I really like the gospel and want to live by the standards of the Church.*

*Going to seminary every morning and having all my good LDS friends with me influences me a lot.*

*Reading the scriptures and seminary help tremendously! Seriously!*

*Seminary is really helping me build up my testimony, and I enjoy going to Church more. The gospel is more interesting to me now, and I am really beginning to understand it.*

*Seminary helps me want to live right!*

These comments confirm what the prophets have declared about why the Lord inspired this program's establishment. "Seminary instruction is one of the most significant spiritual experiences a young woman or man can have," President Ezra Taft Benson declared ("To the Young Women of the Church," *Ensign,* Nov. 1986, p. 82). Similarly, President Spencer W. Kimball taught:

> In my stake conference meetings with bishoprics and stake presidencies and high councils, I have insisted that if they would see that the young people attended the seminaries and institutes, that you would almost guarantee their morality and worthiness, and that they would fill missions, marry in the temple, and live beautiful LDS lives. (*The Teachings of Spencer W. Kimball,* p. 528.)

## *Discourage Youth from Working on Sunday*

The limited social science research that has focused on the influence of high school students working part-time during the school year has generally revealed a modest relationship with delinquency. Several explanations have emerged about why part-time employment increased delinquency among teenagers. First, youth who work part-time jobs spend more time away from the home, which weakens the family's influence on them. It also makes it more difficult for parents to monitor their teen's activities. Becoming friends with fellow workers introduces another peer group that competes for the youth's time and attention. These fellow workers are usually less known to the parents and ofttimes do not have the same values and standards that friends at school and Church may share. Employment also allows teens more independence from their families, and with more money to spend they participate more in leisure activities and entertainment. It is probably a combination of all these factors that slightly increases involvement with inappropriate behaviors when teens hold part-time jobs.

The larger problem for LDS youth and parents, however, is the temptation to work on Sundays. In our experiences as bishops and youth advisers, we have witnessed many active young people slowly drift into inactivity because of jobs that required them to work on the Sabbath. Perhaps for this very reason, the First Presidency and Quorum of the Twelve Apostles, in the *For the Strength of Youth* pamphlet, counseled:

> When seeking a job, you may wish to share with your potential employer your desire to attend your Sunday meetings and keep the Sabbath holy. Many employers value employees with these personal convictions. Try to choose a job that doesn't require you to work on Sunday. (*For the Strength of Youth* [Salt Lake City: The Church of Jesus Christ of Latter-day Saints, 1990], p. 17.)

Some parents may feel that working after school teaches their teens responsibility and also lessens pressures on the family budget. Our advice to parents who desire their children to work is to prayerfully help them carefully choose the job. First, avoid a job that requires working on Sunday and will take the young person away from meaningful Church activity. Second, help them find employment where co-workers, at best, share similar standards, or at least, will not exert negative pressures upon them. Finally, realize that your parental responsibility to monitor and be interested in your child's life will be more difficult with teenage employment. Thus, you must make extra efforts to ensure that having such part-time jobs will actually yield more positive benefits than it may actually cost in detrimental influences.

## Encourage Youth to Gain Their Own Personal Testimony of the Gospel

Perhaps the most important component of the shield of faith is a personal testimony. That is what we as parents want most for our children, for if they possess their own personal, spiritual witness of truth they are more likely to be led to do what is right. As a result, we can see that activity devoid of spiritual substance does not give our youth the strength needed in this day and age to stand firm against the adversary. It may have been possible in generations past to be socially converted to the Church and remain relatively unpolluted by worldly ways. But this is a different day and age. In our own day, we are indeed seeing the fulfillment of the prophecy given by President Heber C. Kimball in the last century:

> To meet the difficulties that are coming, it will be necessary for you to have a knowledge of the truth of this work for yourselves. The difficulties will be of such a character that the man or woman [or youth] who does not possess this personal knowledge will fall. . . . The time will come when no man or woman [or youth] will be able to stand on borrowed light. Each will have to be guided by the light within himself. If you do not have it, how will you stand? (As quoted in Orson F. Whitney, *The Life of Heber C. Kimball,* 1888, reprint [Salt Lake City: Bookcraft, 1967], p. 450.)

All that we do as parents at home and within the programs of the Church to help our youth internalize the gospel culminates in their own personal witness of the truth. Everything else we do outwardly should lead them to a testimony that motivates them inwardly. We can encourage our children to do as Nephi did. After he heard his father recount the vision or dream he had, and after he heard his father expound the gospel and bear testimony, Nephi desired to know for himself. Nephi's faithfulness, spiritual strength, and leadership came not just because of his "goodly parents" who knew the Lord, but also because he too knew for himself (see 1 Nephi 11:1–6). For this reason, we as parents should make this the primary objective of our religious endeavors at home. As one teen in our study said, *"My parents' top priority was that we develop our own personal testimonies."* Several other comments—both by way of positive experience and regrets— from the young adults in the study testify of the power of testimony:

*Looking back now, I wish I would have tried to gain a stronger testimony earlier than I did. It would have given me more strength to rely on.*

*I wish I would have developed a strong testimony real early in life. I found by the time I had strengthened my testimony or experienced my personal conversion, I had already given in to many tempations which I to this day regret. I wish I would have not acted "too cool" for the gospel and instead softened my heart so a testimony could enter in.*

*I wish I would have gained my testimony earlier, so that I would have been able to better overcome temptations and peer pressure. My testimony is now what gives me my strength.*

*A testimony of the Savior and of the gospel's truth is so necessary to resist tempation. In my eyes a testimony is the best prevention against Satan's temptations and is the most important thing parents can teach.*

Personal spirituality—the internalization of gospel principles anchored in a divine witness of the truthfulness of the gospel—is what clothes youth in the "armor of God" and empowers them to "quench the fiery darts of the wicked." At the very center of this must be an understanding and application of the Atonement of Jesus Christ and a testimony of his divinity. This must be the rock foundation on which our teens can build their lives. Only on this foundation can religiosity have any lasting protective power for the youth. As Helaman declared unto his own sons:

> And now, my sons, remember, remember that it is upon the rock of our Redeemer, who is Christ, the Son of God, that ye must build your foundation; that when the devil shall send forth his mighty winds, yea, his shafts in the whirlwind, yea, when all his hail and his mighty storm shall beat upon you, it shall have no power over you to drag you down to the gulf of misery and endless woe, because of the rock upon which ye are built, which is a sure foundation, a foundation whereon if men build they cannot fall (Helaman 5:12).

# 5

# THE FAMILY CONNECTION

## SEEDBED OF STRENGTH

"The home is the seedbed of all true virtue," President Gordon B. Hinckley taught. "If proper values are not learned in the home, they are not likely to be learned anywhere." Prophets of God and religious leaders testify that good homes are the "foundation for the strength of any nation." Similarly, civic leaders, educators, and concerned parents and grandparents see the connection between the family and society. The more the family is connected, the stronger the society. As a result, what parents do within the family unit and how they influence the lives of their children affects far more than those within the walls of their own home. The effects—both good and bad—are far-reaching, both as to space and time. For this very reason, President Hinckley admonished:

> Parents who bring children into the world have a responsibility to love those children, to nurture them and care for them, to teach them those values which would bless their lives so that they will grow to become good citizens. If there is less trouble in the homes, there will be less trouble in the nations. I want to emphasize that

which is already familiar to you, and that is the importance of binding our families together with love and kindness, with appreciation
and respect, and with teaching the ways of the Lord so that your
children will grow in righteousness and avoid the tragedies which
are overcoming so many families across the world. (*Teachings of
Gordon B. Hinckley* [Salt Lake City: Deseret Book Co., 1997], pp.
207–8.)

One of the objectives of our study was to examine the role of the
Latter-day Saint family in helping teens resist temptation and overcome negative peer pressure. We wanted to learn more about what
LDS families are doing in their homes, but more important we
wanted to better understand those parenting strategies that are most
effective in rearing righteous children, as the prophet has charged.

An interesting and somewhat surprising picture of LDS families
emerged from our study. Like the results we have discussed in other
chapters, there was some great news and some news that shows there
is still much room for improvement in many homes. The great news
was the overall strength of LDS families all across the country. A
very high proportion of the teens in our study have two parents, who
were married or sealed in the temple. As can be seen in table 5.1,
over 80 percent of the youth characterized the quality of their parents' marriage as either "very happy" or "happy." This is really good
news. This was very encouraging to us since it shows that relationships between mother and father and between parents and children
are generally warm and supportive. Parents embrace their teenage
children in a loving relationship that includes appropriate parental
guidance. It is within this kind of supportive and loving environment
that parents will be able to have the most influence on their children.

We were amazed at the similarity of LDS families regardless of
where they resided across this land. LDS families are LDS families
no matter their locale! In addition, youth in the Church, wherever

they live, have the same religiosity, function in school in similar ways, and participate in delinquent behaviors at about the same levels. This indicates to us that the doctrines of the Restoration and the religious practices and programs of the Church combine to produce dynamic LDS families regardless of geography. Most important, strong, gospel-centered families can have a powerful influence on the behavior of their teenage children.

Table 5.1 shows the similarities among the LDS families in our studies and highlights some characteristics of the families that—like a glass half-filled with water—can be seen as either positive or negative, or both. It is good news to note that about 60 percent of these families regularly have family prayer. But "the glass is half empty" when you recognize that among the families who were generally quite active in the Church, over a quarter of them rarely, if ever, held family prayer. Similarly, it may seem that the "glass is half full" because over 40 percent regularly hold family home evening. The downside, however, is

## Table 5.1
## Family Religious Practices of LDS Youth (by Region)

| Family Characteristics | East Coast (N=1393) | West Coast (N=632) | Utah Valley (N=1078) |
|---|---|---|---|
| **Family Prayer** | | | |
| Very often/Often | 56% | 62% | 60% |
| Sometimes | 14 | 13 | 13 |
| Rarely/Never | 30 | 25 | 27 |
| **Family Scripture Study** | | | |
| Very often/Often | 26% | 29% | 34% |
| Sometimes | 18 | 19 | 19 |
| Rarely/Never | 56 | 52 | 57 |
| **Family Home Evening** | | | |
| Very often/Often | 44% | 44% | 42% |
| Sometimes | 18 | 17 | 21 |
| Rarely/Never | 38 | 38 | 37 |

that of these families, which may actually have been a more religious sample than the Church in general, almost a like number rarely held family home evenings. Equally distressing is the picture that emerged of the vast majority of these active families (over 70 percent) only sometimes, at best, and rarely or never, at worst, studied the scriptures together as a family. Generally speaking, these results show that we still have work to do to more fully follow the counsel of President Hinckley and his predecessors regarding these important family practices.

The most important and instructive results of our study about the family came from testing the delinquency model shown in figure 5.1 and discussed in chapter 2. The results of testing this model revealed that although the family may not have any direct effects on delinquency, it does have a powerful indirect influence through the selection of friends, resistance to peer pressure, and the internalization of religious principles. Whether there are two parents in the home or whether the mother is employed outside the home are not as significant as three vital parenting practices—*connection, regulation,* and

## Figure 5.1
## Revised Model of Delinquency

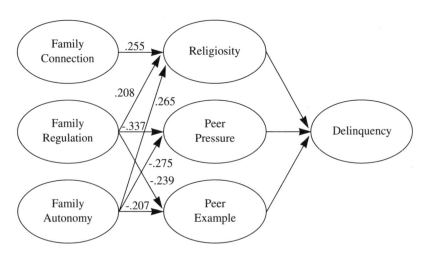

*psychological autonomy.* Parents who despair that their children daily face friends with different standards and who pressure them to violate the standards of the Church, and parents who resent the negative influence of the media—both can use these parenting practices to help their children safely navigate the treacherous waters of adolescence. Those parents who foster feelings of family connectedness; who monitor, regulate, and discipline their children; and who grant them psychological autonomy to have their own thoughts and ideas seem to train teens who do well in school, like and are liked by their peers, who are active in the Church, and who live gospel standards.

## Establishing Family Connectedness

Even though sometimes teens rebuff parental affection and exert their independence, it is crucial that parents establish and maintain warm supportive feelings between their teens and themselves through unfeigned love. *"My parents are very affectionate,"* one fortunate young man stated. *"They always hug me and tell me that they love me. They have often expressed their love for each other and for us in front of all the kids."* Unfortunately, there were some pleas for greater acceptance from parents. *"I wish my parents would respect me more—see me as a person, not as a robot,"* another young man declared. *"I wish I could receive more affection from my dad. Also more encouragement and recognition of my accomplishments and not so much focus on my shortcomings."*

LDS young men and young women's perceptions of their parents' connection to them are presented in table 5.2. The young people living in the Pacific Northwest and in central Utah were asked whether different love-expressing actions were characteristics of their mother or of their father. Youth living along the East Coast are not included in the table because we failed to ask these particular questions of them. As can be seen, over 70 percent of LDS mothers

## Table 5.2
## LDS Youth's Connectedness to Mother and Father
## (By Region)

| My mother (father) is a person who . . . | Mothers | | Fathers | |
|---|---|---|---|---|
| | Pacific Northwest N=636 | Utah Valley N=460 | Pacific Northwest N=636 | Utah Valley N=460 |
| Believes in showing her (his) love for me | 71% | 72% | 57% | 57% |
| Enjoys doing things for me | 70 | 68 | 67 | 63 |
| Smiles at me often | 65 | 67 | 49 | 50 |
| Gives me a lot of attention | 62 | 64 | 47 | 48 |
| Makes me feel better after talking over my worries | 54 | 58 | 35 | 40 |
| Is able to make me feel better when I am upset | 54 | 53 | 40 | 40 |
| Is easy to talk to | 49 | 51 | 30 | 32 |
| Often praises me | 48 | 51 | 38 | 40 |
| Makes me feel like the most important person in her (his) life | 31 | 37 | 38 | 32 |

express their love and seem to enjoy doing things for their children. On the other hand, less than half of the youth report that their mothers are easy to talk to or that their mothers often praise them.

As can be seen in the table, the level of connectedness LDS teens feel with their fathers is lower than that with their mothers. While that is not much different than in society generally, it should cause LDS fathers to pause and consider their relationship with their teens. In recent years many newspaper and magazine articles and television and radio shows have reported the rising rate of "absentee fathers"— homes where children are raised without a father present. While this is a disturbing societal trend, we are also alarmed by the incidence of absentee fathers who are in the home but are absent from the lives of their children. Several young people in the study expressed heartfelt desires that their fathers be more affectionate to them and interested in their lives. *"I wish my dad would have been more involved in my life and had given me a little more praise along with all the responsibilities he put on me,"* one young adult reported. *"I just wish he would have asked me how my day was or how I felt or just talked to me about something besides school and the gospel."* On the positive side, one young woman wrote, *"My dad took me on dates a lot. I know it is important for girls to have a positive relationship with their father. I've seen some of my friends who didn't have a good relationship with their dads turn to boyfriends and pregnancy to fill that void."*

Fulfilling the divine role of fatherhood involves much more than merely providing for the family temporally and being a leader in the home spiritually. It requires emotional involvement, hugs, expressions of love and appreciation, and a commitment of time to be interested and involved in the lives of his children. "A father's duty is to make his home a place of happiness," declared President Ezra Taft Benson. "The powerful effect of righteous fathers in setting an example, disciplining and training, nurturing and loving is vital to the spiritual welfare of his children." He further admonished fathers to do certain, specific things to show their children how much they really love them:

> Go on Daddy-Daughter dates and fathers-and-sons outings with your children. As a family go on campouts and picnics, to ball games and recitals, and to school programs. Having Dad there makes all the difference. . . .
>
> Have regular one-on-one visits with your children. Let them talk about what they want to. Teach them gospel principles. Teach them true values. Tell them you love them. *Personal time with your children tells them where Dad puts his priorities.* (*The Teachings of Ezra Taft Benson,* pp. 509, 511; italics added.)

Although the level of connection between LDS moms and dads and their teenage children is higher than reported by non-LDS parents, there is certainly room for improvement.

Feelings of family connection give youth greater confidence to face their challenges. This connectedness also increases parents' influence in their teenagers' lives since most teens want to please parents who love them and whom they love in return. These feelings of affection and emotional closeness also increase teens' acceptance of regulation and discipline from their parents. Although teens sometimes act as if they want little to do with their family, there are a number of things that parents can do to foster feelings of connectedness between themselves and their children.

## Spend Time with Teens

Family connection requires time, especially one-on-one time. *Newsweek* recently published an article entitled "The Myth of Quality Time" (May 12, 1997; pp. 62–65). The author observed that "kids don't do meetings. You can't raise them in short, scheduled bursts. They need lots of attention." The youth in our study made this point quite vividly in their comments about time they spend with their parents. One young woman articulated her desire for more time with her mother and father. *"I wish my parents would listen to me on an individual basis more, especially when I am having a bad day. I wish they would listen without giving advice, getting upset, or trying to fix the problem. Five to ten minutes of individual one-on-one time makes a big difference."*

An interesting study of over five hundred rural teenagers discovered that well-adjusted youth (didn't smoke, drink, or do drugs and were motivated in school) reported they ate five meals each week on the average with their family as compared to unadjusted teens, who shared only three meals per week with the family. The author pointed out that although it may be that parents don't want to eat with wayward youth, more likely it is that eating together is an indicator of parental time and interest in the lives of their teenagers.

Many of the young people reported that some of their most memorable family experiences were spending time in spontaneous activities with their family, like visiting around the dinner table, running an errand with Dad, or grocery shopping with Mom. One young man told of a time when he had just broken up with his girlfriend. He was sitting on the curb in front of the house feeling quite forlorn and heartbroken. His father noticed him, came out of the house, and sat on the curb with him. His understanding father put his arm around him, hugged him, and then shared an experience from his dating years when he had felt the same kind of pain. In this curbside setting, the young man stated that he could finally *"relate to my dad, and I knew that he knew how I felt. I felt a special closeness to him then."* This son was firmly connected to his family through the love he felt from his father during their spontaneous curbside meeting. That important feeling would then extend into other aspects of the father-son relationship. That one short moment would thereafter affect how the son would respond to his father's teaching and discipline.

Parents are busy. No one doubts this. But, amidst all their busyness, they miss golden opportunities to establish vital connection with their teens if they fail to support them in their school, church, and community activities. A large number of youth indicated great appreciation for their parents' support of their many activities. *"Even though my dad is a very busy man,"* one young man wrote, *"he tries to attend my activities and always makes time for us to do things together as a family."* Other young people expressed disappointment that their parents didn't spend more time with them. For example, one young woman wrote, *"My dad works all the time. It's hard for me to see him a lot. I really would have liked to have spent more time with him."* Another young woman was delighted with her relationship with her mother, but missed ties with her father: *"The only thing I could [have] asked more is of my father, who I respect more than any man alive, but with whom I do not share that same friendship. He was such a busy man that we really didn't spend much time playing together."* Several brothers and sisters made for competition for time with parents in the words of one young woman: *"There are eight kids in our family. Although I know it would be hard, I wish we could have more one-on-one time with our parents."* The youth in the study shared several creative ways their parents spend one-on-one time with them.

*When I was real young (elementary school), my mother had "days" for each of us kids every month. It was our special day to grocery shop with Mom, pick out what we wanted for meals and just our day! As I got older my parents (especially Dad) always came to my softball games and other activities. They showed me that they loved me and wanted me to be happy.*

*My dad would take us kids individually on a "date." We could go wherever we wanted. This used to be McDonald's but now is the Olive Garden. One thing my father does is have an individual interview. He tells us [me] how he feels about me and asks if there is anything wrong and offers to give me a blessing. This is a good thing to do, and I will make sure my future husband does the same.*

*We had "special nights" when we stayed up later than the other kids and did something with Mom and Dad.*

*My mom made lunch for me every day and took me all over for piano lessons, tennis lessons, etc. Also, on my birthday, my parents always went to great lengths to make it a special and fun day for me.*

As is evident from every parent's experience and these comments, raising teenagers is a time-intensive endeavor. Parents must never mistake time in the same room as family togetherness time. Quality family times involve interaction between family members, eyeball-to-eyeball, heart to heart, a complete focusing of attention on each other. Watching a video or TV program together affords only low-level family interaction. Some of the time can be scheduled, such as a father-daughter dinner out, an interview with a son or daughter, or regular family home evening and family prayer. But clearly some of the most valuable time must be given on the spur of the moment when it may be down right inconvenient. Occasions such as visiting with children who have gathered on their parents' bed wanting to talk when parents would rather go to sleep, late night listening to an excited teen who just came in from a date, or joining a dejected son sitting on the curb all demand unplanned parental time, but great are the rewards in family connection.

*Quality time* must also include *quantity time.* To think that sporadic, intense interaction can make up for long periods of limited contact or even neglect is ludicrous. Our children aren't dumb. They know that true quality time must involve a quantity of time, affection, and emotional closeness. To believe otherwise is as silly as the home teacher who does not regularly visit his assigned families but reports, "I have quality visits. I may only visit them once a year, but it is really a good visit."

## Express Your Love to Your Teenagers

Over and over the youth in the study expressed a desire for their parents to tell them more often that they love them. Hearing the words "I love you" can be music to the ears of teens. Expressions of love are as vital to family closeness as a touch, a hug, or a warm smile. Adolescence is a very stressful time, and assurances of love and acceptance are important in order for youth to develop self-confidence. The youth themselves described how much they enjoyed being told by their parents they were loved and reassured that they are acceptable and worthwhile.

*When I was growing up whenever my father took a trip (which was often) he would send me a postcard. It was his way of saying "I love you" and "I am thinking of you." My mom was much more verbal; she would compliment me and encourage me.*

*Both my parents told me they loved me. My mom still kisses me and says she loves me when I see her.*

*My mom is one of my best friends. For example, she knows every single person I've kissed! It is rad! As for my dad, he is a stud. I remember in junior high how I would come home and tell them good night and that I loved them. They would say it back. I don't think these words are ever overused.*

*My parents told me more than three times a day that they love me. We never part at home for the night or hang up the phone without saying I love you. They also showed their love by never holding grudges or throwing past deeds in our faces.*

*My family was never a hugging, touchy-feely family or even a verbal "I love you" family. I can count on one hand the number of times I've hugged my eldest brother. Each time is vividly remembered by me and very important to me. I wish we would show our love more openly.*

*Communication is slim in our family. Rarely do we share our feelings and emotions to each other. There are few I love you's, and it even feels uncomfortable to say it because it is just not spoken.*

*I wish my parents would encourage us to show our feelings more. In my house being emotional is looked down upon, and we have problems expressing our love to each other.*

These last three comments vividly illustrate teens' needs for expressions of love between family members. Parents need to overcome shyness, feelings of embarrassment, or whatever is inhibiting expressions of love between them and their children so that no LDS teen can count on the fingers of one hand the number of times that it has occurred. At times teenagers will act as if such declarations of love embarrass them, but deep inside they feel that special security that comes from being loved. There really is no excuse for parents not expressing their love to their children. Almost every parent has such feelings, and sharing words of love, hugs, and touches take very little time and cost nothing. We promise that good things will come from telling your teens at least once a day that you love them. Don't let them go to bed without their hearing these words or feeling your arms around them.

## *Be Liberal with Praise of Teenagers*

Parents should look for their teens' accomplishments and praise them. Teens thrive on recognition and acceptance, even from parents. Youth in the survey often lamented that they receive a great deal of criticism from their parents about their mistakes, but rare praise for their day-to-day accomplishments. The youth acknowledged their mistakes but were disappointed that their parents directed so much attention to their misdeeds and neglected their accomplishments, albeit they may have been modest. One young man's comment illustrates the emotional and behavioral problems that can occur when a teen feels that he or she doesn't measure up to parental expectations:

*Well, I was kind of emotionally unstable (low self-esteem) due to high expectations in school, Church, and sports. Also, girls not liking me when I liked them and immorality. So I think it would have helped a lot if they [parents] would have made me feel more important and feel successful. Sometimes I felt and still feel, like I can never do anything good enough for my dad. I feel like I never meet his expectations.*

109

As indicated from this young man's perception of his not measuring up to his dad's expectations, parents need to be realistic about their teens' abilities and recognize less than "top of the class" or "best of team" performance. In reality most parents have "average" children, and their averageness should be approved. Sometimes youth may tragically feel that their parents have misunderstood the scripture "If ye are not one, ye are not mine" to mean "If ye are not number one, ye are not mine."

Parents probably praise their teenagers more than their children give them credit for, but all parents find themselves at times being overcritical with teens. Many of the young people saw their mistakes as learning experiences and wanted to put them behind them, but their parents continued to rehash them. Generous praise helps young people to develop the self-esteem or self-confidence that will help them through the difficult teen years and to confidently assume adult roles. It can be discouraging for anyone, but especially teens who naturally struggle with feelings of inadequacy, to feel as if nothing they do is ever good enough. In contrast to continual criticism and an absence of praise, expressions of acceptance are actually motivational. Children who feel praised and recognized for their efforts as well as their deeds try harder to do even better—like the old adage about flies, "You can catch more with honey than vinegar." As Elder H. Burke Peterson testified: "When children and teenagers are loved because of who they are and not for how they behave, only then can we begin to help make much-needed changes in behavior. For example, a teenager who feels accepted will be more likely to choose wholesome friends."

One day after school, one of our daughters came into a teenage son's room. It looked as if a big wind had blown through. He was sitting in the midst of it all. She felt the anger rising within, but remembered her resolution to look for the good. Searching desperately, her eye finally looked upward. "Your ceiling's really clean, Adam!" She was able to say quite honestly. He laughed; he got the message, and he cleaned up the room. (Conference Report, Apr. 1990, p. 106.)

## *Be Generous with Forgiveness*

As teens spread their wings and seek independence from their family, they often make mistakes. Many times their demands for independence get ahead of their good sense, and they do things that try their parents' patience. Parents have an obligation to use such bad decisions or choices as teaching moments, but a spirit of forgiveness and unconditional love are essential to maintaining feelings of family connection. A young woman felt she couldn't talk to her parents about important events in her life because she feared their reaction: *"I wish they would have made it more comfortable to go and talk to them about things. So I wouldn't feel I would get in trouble if I went and talked to them about my problems."* Another youth made a similar comment: *"My parents could have criticized less and tried to help us in our weaknesses, without demeaning us."* One young person's experience humorously demonstrates the importance of parents moving beyond reprimand to empathy and forgiveness:

> *One time I got caught chewing gum in school and had to put a tissue in with the gum and continue to chew it. That night as my dad and I were chatting about personal things (which was rare) I told him what had happened. He immediately took the teacher's side. "You shouldn't have been chewing gum." I knew that! I didn't need him to state the obvious. I needed some sort of thoughtfulness like "I bet that was kind of embarrassing."*

Many teens acknowledged in various ways that they often make mistakes but are disappointed that their parents keep bringing them up long after they have occurred. Parents probably want to remind their teenagers not to make the same mistake twice, but teens see repeated references to past foibles as limiting their growing up and not putting past mistakes behind them. They also feel that recounting earlier mistakes conveys a lack of empathy and trust. Empathy and associated forgiveness means a lot to young people. One young woman's comments illustrate her appreciation of her parents' empathy with her mistakes and problems: *"I know my parents feel my pain. I know it hurts them when I am hurting and this touches me."* At some point, parents need to write "finished," "over and done with," "forgiven and forgotten" on the ledger of their children's mistakes. President J. Reuben Clark Jr. often stated his belief that when it came time for judgment, the Savior will extend the *maximum* amount of mercy possible and exact the *minimum* degree of justice allowable. Perhaps parents could use this divine equation in dealing with their children.

## *Develop Family Traditions*

Special birthday celebrations, family vacations, conference watching sessions, family home evenings, and similar traditions help to connect teenagers to their families. Long after they have forgotten much about their teenage years, individuals recall with nostalgia participating in family traditions. Often such traditions are passed on from one generation to the next. These traditions of family closeness need not be formal or reserved only for holidays or special occasions. Sometimes the most meaningful to youth are the most informal. For example, a young adult remembered the "family film festival":

> *One of my favorite times with my family was when we had a day off from school and if the weather was bad we would spend the day watching our favorite videos. We would all stay in our pajamas*

*and cuddle up together on the floor under quilts or on the bean-bag chairs and watch movies. Every kid got to choose his or her favorite movie. Dad would buy treats and Mom popped popcorn. I can't even remember the movies, but I remember the fun we had. We got so that we almost hoped for bad weather sometimes so we could have our "family film festival."*

Another young woman spoke with fondness of the times her father would check her out of school to go skiing with him. *"The time I spent with him in the chairlift was some of the most meaningful time I have ever had in life."*

It is amazing what our grown-up children remember from their childhoods—silly Christmas nativity pageants, building houses with Lego blocks while watching general conference on television, going for root beer after Little League games. The list could go on and on. Wonderful memories sometimes are made by happenstance, but often they must be made by conscientious efforts to develop warm and loving traditions of family togetherness.

## Give Father's Blessings

The start of a new school year, a special athletic contest, an important musical performance, a dating relationship, contemplation of a mission, or times of discouragement are significant opportunities for parents to demonstrate their love and concern for their teenage children. One youth's comment illustrates the desire for father's blessings: *"I wish my father would offer to give me a blessing at least once a year instead of me always having to ask, which I don't do very often."* While serving as bishops we were a little surprised to discover in the course of our interviews how few youth mentioned that they had received blessings at the hands of their fathers. When youth confided in an interview they were struggling with a problem, we would often ask whether they had received a blessing from their father. Rarely did they respond in the affirmative and often a bishop's blessing was substituted. We always encouraged these youth to ask their fathers for a blessing. From our limited experience, we suspect that fathers are not availing themselves as often as they should of this wonderful opportunity to express their love to their children by calling down the blessings of heaven into their lives. Youth welcome this support and thereby draw closer to their family and their Heavenly Father. Often these moments are among the most spiritually instructive in their lives. Sometimes even more important than what is said in the blessing is the feeling of spiritual intimacy that brings moms, dads, and children closer together and closer to the Lord.

When speaking publicly about fathers' blessings, we have joked with our audiences that such blessings don't count unless they are "sealed" with a hug. There is probably no more significant time for a father to hold a teenage daughter or son in his arms and express his love and appreciation than after he has pronounced an inspired blessing on his beloved child. Those are important moments not to be missed.

## Love and Honor Your Spouse

One final point we wish to make about family connection may seem off the point, but it is significant. Family closeness involves more than just the parent-child relationships. It is directly linked to the husband-wife relationship. Several youth mentioned how difficult it was to feel close to their parents when they witnessed criticism, arguing, and conflict between Mom and Dad. We asked the youth three questions about how often they saw their parents nagging and complaining about each other, arguing, and yelling or screaming at each other. The results for youth living in the Pacific Northwest and in Utah are presented in table 5.3. As can be seen, about a third of the

# Table 5.3
# Family Conflict Perceived by LDS Youth, by Region

| Family Conflict | Pacific Northwest (N=632) | Utah Valley (N=1078) |
|---|---|---|
| **My parents nag and complain about each other around the house** | | |
| Not true | 65% | 62% |
| Somewhat true | 27 | 31 |
| True | 8 | 7 |
| | | |
| **I often see my parents arguing** | | |
| Not true | 68% | 63% |
| Somewhat true | 24 | 27 |
| True | 8 | 10 |
| | | |
| **My parents often yell and scream at each other when I'm around** | | |
| Not true | 84% | 81% |
| Somewhat true | 11 | 13 |
| True | 6 | 5 |

young people notice nagging and complaining or see their parents arguing. About 15 percent actually witness with some degree of frequency their parents yelling and screaming at one another.

A substantial number of young people commented that such tension between parents interfered with their feeling of connection with them.

*I wish my parents could have loved each other more as I was growing up. As a teenager, my eyes were opened to how imperfect they are. The disrespect they had for each other, no matter how much they respected me, taught me to disrespect them in many ways. I wish they would promote more love in the family.*

*My dad sometimes gets ornery with my mom over stupid little things, and this bothers me.*

*I wish my parents would spend more time together, not fight as much, and attend the temple more often.*

Even when parents try to keep their differences behind closed doors, their teenage children sense things are not right. They note the lack of loving glances and expressions of appreciation, the tight-lipped replies, and the cold silence. Obviously parents do have their moments of disagreement, but these need to be resolved and peace quickly restored in the home.

In contrast, several of the young people spoke of how much it meant to them to hear their parents express love to each other and show that love through tenderness and expressions of affection. "Fathers, express your love for your wife and children," President Howard W. Hunter admonished. "You should express regularly to your wife and children your reverence and respect for her. Indeed, one of the greatest things a father can do for his children is to love their mother." (*The Teachings of Howard W. Hunter,* ed. Clyde J. Williams [Salt Lake City: Bookcraft, 1997], p. 152.) Certainly President Hunter's prophetic counsel applies as much to mothers as fathers.

The loving relationship between parents and teenage children creates special feelings of being accepted and belonging that is so essential to teens. A home with a high level of family connectedness is the ideal environment for parents to then regulate the children's behavior. President Joseph F. Smith perhaps said it best:

If you will keep your [children] close to your heart, within the clasp of your arms; if you will make them . . . feel that you love them . . . and keep them near to you, they will not go very far from you, and they will not commit any very great sin. But it is when you turn them out of your home, turn them out of your affection . . . that [is what] drives them away from you.

... if you wish your children to be taught in the principles of the gospel, if you wish them to love truth and understand it, if you wish them to be obedient to and united with you, love them! and prove . . . that you do love them by your every word and act to[ward] them." (*Gospel Doctrine,* 5th ed. [Salt Lake City: Deseret Book Co., 1966], pp. 282, 316.)

## Regulating and Monitoring Behavior

Regulation involves three activities on the part of parents. The first is to establish, with their children's input, family rules or principles that will guide their family life. Second, parents must monitor their teenagers' compliance with those family rules and guiding principles. The third task is perhaps the most painful for parents—administering appropriate discipline when rules are broken or principles defied.

How LDS parents are monitoring their teens' behavior, one important aspect of regulation, is presented in table 5.4. Previous studies have discovered that researchers do not need to ask about all three regulation activities as those parents who monitor their teens also set rules and administer discipline. Thus this table reports only monitoring. In our study, the youth reported what they believed their mothers and fathers really know about five important areas of their lives. As can be seen, mothers know pretty much where their teens are after school and in the evening. A little over 60 percent know who their teenage children hang out with, while about 55 percent are aware how the young people spend their free time. Interestingly, less than half of the mothers really know on what the young people spend their money. Fathers leave the major responsibility of monitoring their teenagers' behavior to the mothers as significantly fewer fathers are knowledgeable about the where, with whom, and whats of their children's lives.

## Table 5.4
## LDS Youth's Perceptions of Parental Regulation
## (By Region)

| My mother (father) is a person who knows . . . | Mothers | | Fathers | |
|---|---|---|---|---|
| | East Coast N=636 | Utah Valley N=460 | East Coast N=636 | Utah Valley N=460 |
| Where I am after school | 80% | 74% | 45% | 39% |
| Where I go at night | 74 | 72 | 52 | 47 |
| Who my friends are | 61 | 63 | 31 | 34 |
| What I do with my free time | 57 | 55 | 39 | 34 |
| How I spend my money | 47 | 48 | 27 | 27 |

Considerable social-psychological research over the years has demonstrated that youth who grow up in homes without specific rules and regulations for their behavior and who are not held accountable, fail to learn to control their own behavior. They lack that self-control that is so critical for success in all of life's endeavors. Lacking self-control, such youth often act impulsively and do things they later regret and that may harm themselves and others along the way. In addition, they are overly susceptible to influence from peers, which often results in participation in activities they normally would avoid.

The bottom line is that if parents don't teach their children self-control through appropriate regulation, then they had better hope that public school teachers and Church leaders do it for them or eventually the police and courts will be forced to do so. Adulthood requires that individuals take responsibility for their actions. Those who don't learn this in their youth will receive their training from the "school of hard knocks." In extreme cases, we are aware of young people who end up spending a couple years of their lives in prison learning this essential lesson rather than being in the mission field or receiving a college education. The following practical suggestions may help parents in the difficult task of regulating the behavior of their teenage children. Successful regulation will contribute to a more loving, peaceful family life and to the development of self-control in the individual.

## *Establish Family Rules*

Teens need the structure provided by family rules, values, or principles. They need guidance in appropriately expressing their growing independence and freedom. The number and formality of family rules can vary from two or three guiding principles to a multi-page detailed family constitution. The format is not as important as building family, Church, and school expectations into the family rules. Treating all family members with respect, working hard for good grades in school, regular attendance at Church meetings, and adherence to the Word of Wisdom are examples. It is important that teens have input into both the rules and the associated discipline or punishment. Family councils are opportunities to discuss the reasons underlying each rule and to negotiate appropriate punishment for non-compliance. One young woman described this process in her family:

*My parents let us make our own rules. For example, we chose a curfew and a punishment for breaking it. We, as a family, but mostly the daughters, picked a curfew of 10:30 on weeknights, 1:00 A.M. on Friday nights and midnight on Saturday nights. If we were even one minute late we got punished. The established punishment was for every minute we were late, we lost one hour from our next date. It was what we chose.*

We were surprised at the number of youth who in their written comments requested greater parental regulation in their life. For example, one young woman lamented, *"In my family there is too much freedom!!! I miss out on some spiritual restrictiveness.*" Two young men voiced similar sentiments:

> *Sometimes I wish my parents were more strict. I wish they were more like parents and less like my buddies. Sometimes you just need a parent to put their foot down instead of always saying "What you think is all right with me."*

> *It is hard to say this, but it's probable that they were too lenient on me with punishment. Sometimes they were giving and bendable and if they would have been a little more stern with punishment I feel I would have gained a greater respect for rules and living standards of the home.*

Another young woman had the all too frequent problem of inconsistency between Mom and Dad in their regulation. *"I wish my dad would be more lenient and my mom more strict so I could in turn respect them."* It is amazing to hear teenagers ask their parents to establish and enforce more strict yet fair rules. Popular rhetoric occasionally encourages parents to abandon their parental roles and seek more to be their children's friends. Teenagers generally have enough friends; what they need are two concerned parents who will lovingly yet consistently guide them through the trials and difficulties of adolescence.

As mentioned previously, it is imperative that teenagers feel some degree of ownership in family rules. Several youth in our study noted they had to really exert themselves to have even minimal influence on family rules. *"We have a family constitution which dictates all of our rules,"* one young man noted and then added, *"I had to fight for any input!"* A young woman shared a similar account: *"It isn't often that we (the children) are decision makers in family matters or have a say or vote about family rules. I wish they wouldn't always take the 'I'm the parent, you are the kid' attitude."*

Even though they chafe against family rules, most teens recognize that regulation is for their own good. A young woman clearly articulated this awareness: *"It was very clear that if we want to enjoy freedom there are guidelines we need to operate within. We are punished if we go against the rules, yet these rules allow us to have maximum freedom."*

When children, especially teenagers, have some input into the family rules and the punishments for disobedience, it becomes more difficult to fight against the rules or resent the consequences. As one young man observed, *"It's pretty hard for me to rebel against my parents, since I helped make the rules for the family!"*

One final comment about family rules. A number of young people reported they used family rules and their parents as "excuses" to avoid activities they didn't feel good about. An appeal to "unreasonable" parents allows these young men and women to walk away from delinquent and immoral activities without losing face and without eliciting the wrath or ridicule of their peers.

## *Monitor Teenagers' Behavior*

Once family rules, principles, guidelines, and punishments have been fairly, not arbitrarily, established, parents ultimately have the responsibility to assess compliance. In some respects monitoring is even more important than rules. If a family has a zillion rules yet parents do not actively monitor their children, the rules are meaningless. Many of the young people in our study stated that they had very few family rules, but that their parents were very informed and involved in their lives. *"My parents allowed me quite a lot of freedom,"* one young man reported, *"but they insisted on knowing where I was going and who I was with."* As can be seen in this comment, the best way for monitoring to be done is for parents to talk with their teenagers. This can be done by simply asking questions like "Where are you going?" "Who are you going with?" "When will you be back?" and "Is your homework done?" The best information gathering question we found with our own teenage children has been, "Do you have enough money?" Seizing upon an opportunity for a little extra, they almost always answered "no." Although it ended up costing us a few extra dollars, it provided us excellent opportunity to learn where our children were going and what they would be doing. Sometimes our teens balked at revealing where they were going and we would jokingly reply, "What if some good-looking young woman (or young man for our daughters) calls for you? How will I know where to forward the call? If I don't know where you will be, you really will miss out." With that, they would laughingly open up about their plans.

When the bonds of family connection are strong, youth tend not to lie to their parents. However, if parents become concerned that their teens are not being truthful with them, they should check with parents of friends or with teachers. It is not "spying" or "invading privacy"—it is merely fulfilling a vital parental role of monitoring. Parents should always be alert for obvious signs of trouble in their kids' lives. A significant decline in school performance, complaints from teachers and school officials, declining Church involvement, new friends, staying out unusually late at night, and sudden personality changes are signals that all is not well with the young person. We are not suggesting that parents become overly intrusive in their teenage children's lives; rather, that they not neglect their responsibility to provide the guidance their children need and deserve. The comments of two young women illustrate how their parents monitored their behavior.

*My parents always wanted to know where I was going, what I was doing, and who I was with. They were always aware of what was happening in my life because they were my best friends. Every*

122

*night before I went to bed, I would go to their room and talk about my life and any concerns I may have had. My parents always knew what was going on in my life.*

*My parents always wanted to meet our friends. They often made it a point to meet their parents as well. They helped us budget our money and kept track of how we spent it. They constantly gave us advice.*

## Enforce Compliance to Family Rules

Now comes the hard part of regulation—the dispensing of discipline. Parents want to have friendly, fun relations with their children, and disciplining them threatens this. Disciplining teenagers is difficult, but it is critical if teens are to learn that their behavior has consequences. Discipline or punishment when rules or principles are broken is necessary for teens to learn the important lesson they are responsible for their actions in the home, the school, the neighborhood, and the Church. Out of an aversion to disciplining children and fear that such discipline may endanger family closeness, some parents live with the hope that the bishop might be inspired to call a "ward disciplinarian." Perhaps the bishop would call the toughest member of the ward—maybe a retired Army drill sergeant. Then parents could send their wayward teens over to the church meetinghouse one evening each week so this person could administer the necessary discipline. We all know that this won't happen; in the meantime, the responsibility to discipline remains on the shoulders of parents where it rightfully belongs.

We asked a large number of BYU students to think back to when they were in high school and to report the activities for which their parents disciplined or punished them. The most frequently mentioned behavior to draw parental ire was staying out too late, violating curfew, or failing to call when they were going to be late getting home. Staying out too late was followed in frequency of discipline by arguing or fighting with their brothers and sisters. In defense of their sibling conflicts, many of the youth complained they were unfairly disciplined by their parents for disputes with younger siblings who were "really" at fault. The third most frequently described behavior that elicited parental discipline was disrespect for their parents, such as sassing or talking back to their mother or father. Not doing assigned chores was also a source for disciplinary action. Finally, school problems, such as bad grades, too many absences, and calls from teachers were reported as a source of discipline. Below are a few responses to the question "What were the things you did that you were disciplined or punished for by your parents?"

*Breaking curfew, not doing chores at home, not letting parents know where I was, being impatient with my younger sister.*

*Staying out after my established curfew, but most importantly, not calling if I was staying out or going to be late.*

*Lying about my actual whereabouts, staying out past curfew, and backtalking to my parents.*

*Staying out too late (past curfew) was worthy of extensive punishment. Most of all, deceiving my parents elicited the greatest punishment (ie., telling them I would be one place and doing something else).*

*Fighting with my sisters, staying out too late, and getting bad grades.*

*I got the most punishment when I stayed out later than I was supposed to. I also got into trouble a lot for fighting with my brother. Also, talking back to or "sassing" my mother.*

These young BYU students described the type of discipline they received from their parents, and grounding was by far the most frequent punishment. Generally, grounding involved forbidding the teen from going out in the evening with friends, which to most teens is a fate worse than death. Sometimes grounding included restricting access to the family automobile. The second most frequently used punishment was withholding important privileges such as watching TV, listening to music, or talking on the telephone. Some parents added extra work, like doing dishes or cleaning as punishment for inappropriate behavior. A substantial number of young people reported their parents yelled or shouted at them as their primary form of discipline. Finally, a few teens indicated their parents used psychological punishment to discipline them. These parents induced feelings of guilt in their teenage children by refusing to talk to them or to interact with them. Only a very small number of teens mentioned they received physical punishment, slapping, or hitting. Typical responses are:

*They yelled, screamed, hollered, and occasionally slapped me.*

*I either was grounded, couldn't drive my car, or I wouldn't get my allowance.*

*Yelling and grounding were done, but the grounding was often forgotten about. Taking away the use of the car was a common punishment. Mostly, it was just the fact that my dad would not let tensions die for a few days. So I felt miserable and didn't want to do things that would cause him to react that way.*

*Gave me the usual lecture about responsibility, then grounded me for the weekend or had me wash dishes extra nights besides my turn (which they rarely followed through on) or grounded me from reading my novels.*

*They gave me a guilt trip that I think was worse than other punishment.*

*My mom would ask me why I did it and tell me why I was given a curfew, then privileges of going out would be taken away. Dad would get upset and not say anything, but would give me looks that could pierce anyone's heart. Sometimes he would say that he was disappointed in me (which is worse than hitting).*

*When my mom gets mad at me she gets really silent and refuses to talk to me.*

We were surprised at how infrequently these youth reported their parents had disciplined them during their high school years. Two-thirds of the teens indicated their parents administered punishment only a few times per year. The responses of the other third of the students were evenly divided between those disciplined about once a month, twice a month, or at least once a week. When we first looked at this finding we thought that LDS parents are wimps, lacking the strength to administer appropriate punishment. Closer examination of the responses revealed these BYU students reported that overall they were pretty good kids and really did not need or deserve regular discipline. Some sample comments about how often their parents disciplined them are:

*Less than once a year. I hated being in trouble and would never do anything on purpose that I knew would anger my parents.*

*Once every two months. I was a good kid, with or without their discipline.*

*About once a month. I was a pretty good kid.*

*Honestly, I'd have to say that I rarely did anything that warranted serious discipline, so maybe once or twice a year I would get punished.*

Finally, we asked the students whether they felt the punishment they had received was fair and fit the crime. The vast majority acknowledged their parents had been very fair in their discipline. Many realized their parents had punished them out of love. For example, one young woman wrote: *"I have come to know how hard it is to punish the ones you love. My parents let me know all the time that they wished they didn't have to take away privileges."* A few young people complained their parents were too strict or that they were disciplined more often than a brother or sister. But many more of the young people wished their parents had disciplined them more often and more severely. Below are several typical comments:

*Often I felt I should have been punished for some of the things I did. I often felt I was not cared about because I was not punished for anything. I also had no rules or chores. I felt that they just didn't care what I did, which in many instances they didn't. My parents were too wrapped up in their own lives.*

*I think my mom should have punished me more, maybe by grounding because I was never grounded in my life. She could have taken away a privilege in order for me to learn a lesson. I never really was punished in my life.*

*My parents should have stuck to their punishment. They always let me off the hook early. I think it would have been more effective if they wouldn't have done that.*

*When they threatened me with a punishment, they should have followed through. Usually they backed down.*

Prior to analyzing the discipline reported by these students we were concerned about needing to encourage parents to administer more punishment as part of the regulation of their teenagers. Our feelings about the importance of appropriate discipline have not changed, but it appears that LDS youth really are pretty good kids and do not require a great deal of punishment. These BYU students perhaps were a little more academically inclined in high school and didn't get in trouble quite as much as other teens, but even so, their responses indicate LDS teens commit behavior that require discipline fairly infrequently. Parents can relax while they discipline their teenage children, as the teens expect it and realize that they deserve it. Importantly, it appears from these comments that the discipline doesn't need to be an emotionally draining experience. Rather, a calm discussion and appropriate grounding or forfeiture of privileges is all that is necessary. The students repeatedly requested their parents to forego the yelling, the guilt trips, and the silent treatment, and instead to calmly decree the length of the grounding or the privilege to be given up. Interestingly, almost all the youth whose parents had used the guilt or silent treatment as punishment, noted that such was not appropriate nor was it necessary. They felt this punishment damaged the relationship between themselves and their parents.

In short, parents can take heart—teenage children generally require only relatively infrequent discipline or punishment and expect and accept as fair most discipline. Grounding or taking away privileges appears to be effective disciplinary techniques that can be administered with minimal tension or conflict between parent and youth.

Parents need to quietly yet firmly discuss each violation of a rule and explain the impact such behavior has on the teen and those with whom he or she associates. Then the appropriate discipline needs to be discussed. Agreement about the length of restriction or the nature of the privileges to be forfeited may not come easily, but at least the teen has had an opportunity to express his or her feelings about what is appropriate. Furthermore, unity between Mom and Dad in parental discipline is crucial in order that teens are not able to play one parent against the other.

## *Show Increased Love Following Discipline*

Not surprising, teens often view discipline or punishment as rejection by their parents. Sometimes parents exaggerate the severity of the tension between them and their wayward teenager by inducing feelings of guilt. Excessive guilt induction is not good: the reasons why will be discussed in the next section on psychological autonomy. The scriptures teach a valuable eternal law that when it is necessary to discipline someone we love that we should show forth increased love lest they esteem us their enemy (see D&C 121:43–44). Expressions of love and forgiveness, coupled with invitations to family activities, will restore feelings of family connectedness. Increased love after discipline will lend itself far greater to behavioral changes than punishment alone. "Nothing is so calculated to lead people to forsake sin as to take them by the hand and watch over them in tenderness," the Prophet Joseph Smith instructed. "When persons manifest the least kindness and love to me, O what power it has over my mind, while the opposite course has a tendency to harrow up all the harsh feelings and depress the human mind." (*History of the Church* 5:23–24.)

## *Assign All Family Members Household Chores*

It may seem somewhat off the subject, but giving chores for children to do in the family is directly linked to family regulation. In a way it becomes the lab experience in the family school where parents are teaching lessons about responsibility and accountability. Completing assignments around the home helps children develop a sense of responsibility. It also can serve to teach all members of the family how their behavior has consequences for others. Having responsibility for washing dishes, cleaning a room, mowing the lawn, or tending a younger brother or sister teaches responsibility. If a meal is delayed because of insufficient clean dishes, the unreliable teen learns a valuable lesson. Once chores are assigned, parents need to ensure that teens complete their assigned tasks. This parental responsibility will not only have immediate effects on the daily life of the family but will also yield long-term dividends in the lives and character of the children. "Children need to be taught the joy of honest labor and experience the satisfaction which results from seeing a job well done," Elder L. Tom Perry declared.

I am shocked as I become aware that in so many homes, many of the children do not know how to make a bed, care for their clothing, squeeze a tube of toothpaste to conserve, turn off the lights, set a proper table, mow a lawn, or care for a vegetable garden. These simple acts of cleanliness, order, and conservation will bless their lives every day they live and prepare them to become self-sufficient when they reach an age when they must be out on their own. (Conference Report, Oct. 1988, pp. 87–88.)

Teaching responsibility and accountability in the home can be done better in practice and through chores and tasks than merely in theory by talking about it or teaching abstract lessons on the subject. It is a vital parental obligation that cannot be neglected. A young woman illustrated this point as she expressed her disappointment with her father for failing to check up on her assignment:

*I know I would have far more respect for my parents if they more clearly set boundaries for me. For instance, I recall my dad repeatedly told me to do my job for the week, the dishes. I kept putting them in the back of my mind, not wanting to do them. My dad gave up and did them himself. I remember being frustrated at him for not setting his foot down and demanding that I heed him despite the fact that I didn't want to do them.*

Undoubtedly this father thought he was doing his daughter a kindness. At the time she probably was delighted that she had escaped doing her assigned chore and could spend more time watching television. The wisdom wrought by three more years of maturity enabled her to realize that her loving father had not done her any favor. She realized that there are times in life when an individual needs to serve others regardless of whether they want to or whether it is convenient.

# Granting Psychological Autonomy

Psychological autonomy begins with parents encouraging teenagers to express their own ideas, feelings, opinions, and perceptions within a context of mutual respect. If parents react aghast when a teen expresses an idea that may seem "off the wall," the child may clam up and not share his or her feelings with parents. Psychological autonomy is essential for youth to develop an individual identity, a sense of personal competency, and feelings of self-worth. This can be a hard concept for parents to grasp. It is not merely allowing teens to exercise their agency. This falls under the category of parental regulation. *Psychological autonomy concerns thoughts, ideas, opinions, and feelings, not behaviors or actions.*

Psychological autonomy is generally measured by asking youth how their parents try to control their behavior, with special attention given to love withdrawal and heavy guilt induction. The frequency that LDS youth reported their parents use inappropriate disciplinary tactics is presented in table 5.5. The table reports the percentage of mothers and fathers who *don't regularly* use these means to control their children. Tragically, still about a third of the mothers and fathers withdraw their attention and affection from teenagers who do things with which they disagree. For example, over 30 percent of the youth reported their mothers stop talking to them when they have hurt their mother's feelings. Although these levels of granting

## Table 5.5
## LDS Youth's Perception of Psychological Autonomy
## (By Region)

| My mother (father) is a person who does not . . . | Mothers | | Fathers | |
|---|---|---|---|---|
| | East Coast N=636 | Utah Valley N=460 | East Coast N=636 | Utah Valley N=460 |
| Stop talking to me until I please her (him) again | 69% | 69% | 74% | 74% |
| Avoid looking at me when I have disappointed her (him) | 67 | 65 | 68 | 67 |
| Always try to change me | 67 | 64 | 70 | 67 |
| Say if I really cared for her (him), I would not do things that cause her (him) to worry | 63 | 62 | 70 | 68 |
| Only keep rules when it suits her (him) best | 61 | 56 | 61 | 57 |
| Want to control whatever I do | 60 | 63 | 61 | 62 |
| Act less friendly to me if I do not see things her (his) way | 52 | 50 | 51 | 48 |
| Want to be able to tell me what to do all the time | 52 | 55 | 53 | 54 |
| Always tell me how I should behave | 37 | 36 | 42 | 40 |
| Tell me all the things she (he) has done for me | 31 | 30 | 42 | 37 |

psychological autonomy are reasonably high compared to other studies, it is clear that LDS parents have room to improve.

Youth who are denied psychological autonomy by their parents come to feel the only way to please their parents is to give up their individuality and be exactly what the parents expect them to be. Under these circumstances teens fail to learn to trust their own thoughts, feelings or perceptions; thus they remain overly dependent on their parents. Because such teens lack confidence in their own ideas and feelings, they tend to withdraw inside themselves and develop emotional problems like depression, eating disorders among young women, and in some cases thoughts of suicide. A young woman attending BYU explained how she was denied psychological autonomy and the consequences:

> One of my parents was very domineering and opinionated in many respects. If you disagreed with them, get ready to have a debate to the death or give up to avoid the trouble. I didn't feel like open opinions were welcome. There was one "right" opinion and you better be sure yours matched it. It took coming to college to learn the true meaning of freedom of expression and thought.

Other youth reported similar struggles with psychological autonomy:

> I hate how my dad won't listen to anything I say—my ideas, expressions, just because I am a "kid."

> Dad was opinionated, felt he was right almost always. He is also very smart and so when I presented a different viewpoint or argument, he would always swat it down. I don't think that he ever took me very seriously. His opinions ended up being mine.

> Any opinion different from my dad's was considered unrighteous. He had a gospel answer for any controversy or idea. Any character trait different than what he thought he had was unrighteous.

> I don't think I developed independence, my own ideas, or any self-identity until I moved out of the house and was living on my own.

> Well, my dad is incredibly smart and he has a "red" personality, if you know what I mean. So to have a different opinion was almost committing suicide. It wasn't too bad, though, he was always right.

*My parents aren't always very understanding. Sometimes there is something that I really want to do and they say no before hearing the whole story. I wish they would have a more open relationship with me instead of an authoritarian one.*

*My parents are extremely controlling. They always had a say in everything I did. So now that I am older, it's hard to make a decision without asking my parents what they think.*

Since this is a difficult concept to understand, we presented several of these statements from the youth to illustrate how parents fail to allow their teenage children sufficient psychological autonomy. One more example from a current BYU student who describes an event that happened way back in the sixth grade (obviously, it was important to him as he still remembers it with considerable emotion):

*My parents often discouraged ideas or plans that they deemed impractical. I wish they would have supported some of my fanciful and impractical ideas. It would have shown me that they trusted my judgment and loyalty to good principles. In some ways I wish they would have let me take more chances. Like when I was in the sixth grade I was frustrated with my paper route. I told my parents I wanted to quit and write a book to make money. My mom said that was a foolish idea. I wish she would have entertained the idea and encouraged me to take risks like writing a book.*

We understand the mother labeling the boy's idea about making money from writing a book as foolish. But rather than simply dismissing it, she should have discussed it with him and helped him understand how much hard work it takes to write a book and even whether he had anything to say in a book for which people would be willing to pay.

On the other hand, a young woman recounted how her parents fostered psychological autonomy and the positive consequences for her.

> *We talked about* everything—*politics, literature, religion, sports, cartoons, etc. We were almost encouraged to disagree and form our own opinions. My dad sort of "baited" us into arguing with him. Even if we disagreed at the end, it was okay. The bottom line for everything was (after discussion) what would be the* best/right *decision. That became* my *decision.*

This father may have gone a little too far in "baiting" his teenage children to argue with him, but it seems that he at least used the opportunity to help his children arrive at a "best" or "right" idea, opinion, or decision, hopefully consistent with gospel principles. Youth (indeed all of us) respond better to discussion and discovering the implications for themselves than when they feel it is jammed down their throats. We hope the contrast between the descriptions about their interaction with their parents of these two youth is clear. In the first case, the teenager was not allowed the opportunity to express his or her own ideas and thus developed limited confidence in his or her own abilities. On the other hand, the second family encouraged their teenagers to explore different ideas and to match them with important moral, ethical, and family values. These young people gained confidence in their own ideas, opinions, and feelings.

From the results of this study, the comments of hundreds of youth, and our own experiences, we have discovered that there are a number of specific things parents can do to foster psychological autonomy in their teenage children.

## *Encourage Your Teenagers to Share Their Feelings, Opinions, Hopes, and Desires*

Asking a teenager what he or she thinks about a specific gospel principle, a family rule, an event that happened at school, the national news, the message in a television program or movie, or the lyrics of a popular song will elicit interesting ideas, opinions, and perceptions. It is important that parents listen with genuine interest and respect and not interrupt their teen. In other words, parents must give their children the opportunity to fully express themselves in a friendly environment. Parents need to make sure all children in the family have their turn in expressing themselves without fear of humiliation or intimidation.

## *Express Acceptance of Your Teenager's Attitudes, Opinions, or Feelings, Even If You Disagree with Them*

Teens are fairly sensitive to ridicule and criticism and likely will close up and remain silent if Mom and Dad react with displeasure at some of their ideas. Don't "freak out" to your kids' off-the-wall ideas or wacky opinions. As any parent will testify, teens often do have what seem to parents to be weird perceptions of the world. In spite of such feelings on the part of parents, they need to recognize the youth's ability to have their own ideas about the world. Confidence to share ideas and feelings with parents is critical to the development of a competent young adult.

Young people who feel their ideas, thoughts, and feelings have been minimized, ignored, or outright ridiculed by their parents may seek out a peer group that will listen and give credibility to their opinions and feelings. Parents need not agree with or accept everything, but it is better to allow for the free expression of ideas and discuss them and their implications than to squash them out of hand.

Suppressing psychological automony often makes a teen feel forced to rebel so he or she can express themselves.

## *Help Your Teenage Children to Explore the Source of Their Attitudes, Feelings, or Ideas and Their Consequences*

Once a parent has calmly listened to their teenage daughter or son's ideas or feelings, they are in a position to lead the teen in a discussion of why they feel or believe the way they do. "That is an interesting idea, why do you believe that. . . ?" is one way to initiate such a dialogue. Questions such as "What if everyone felt that way or believed that?" will encourage youth to think about the consequences of their ideas. Within the context of such a discussion parents should share their feelings, ideas, and opinions and why they feel or believe the way they do. This is the ideal setting to teach values and principles consistent with the gospel. Subtle guidance and gentle persuasion will often nurture attitudes and feelings in teens that parents desire. Never allowing the child to express and explore his or her ideas closes lines of communication and prevents meaningful parental guidance from occurring.

## *Allow Your Teenage Children the Opportunity to Be Their Own Persons*

It is sometimes difficult, but always important, for parents to not impose themselves on their teens. In other words, parents should not try to relive their lives and satisfy their unfulfilled dreams through the lives of their children. Playing on the basketball team, participating in the school band, or being a cheerleader may have been a life or death issue to parents in their youth, but their children may not have the same interests or abilities. The Texas mother who hired someone to kill the mother of a teen her daughter was competing against to be a cheerleader is an extreme example of a parent imposing her dreams on her daughter.

To a lesser degree, but indicative of the same problem, we are all familiar with fathers who become obsessed with making their sons into star football, basketball, baseball, or golf stars. It becomes a way for a parent to fulfill his or her lost dreams, but often at the expense of a close relationship with the child. Parents certainly should encourage their children to participate in such wholesome activities and make available the opportunity to do so, but then allow them to make the decision as to what they like and what they really want to do. The idea is for parents to help their teenage children become confident in their own abilities in order to understand their world and know how to live in it so they can accomplish their own dreams or goals in life.

## *Don't Use Love Withdrawal or Excessive Guilt as a Means to Change Inappropriate Behaviors, Opinions, or Feelings*

Unfortunately, many parents discover that the threat of withdrawing love is a powerful force that can be used to control children. "Go to your room—I can't stand the sight of you" or "I don't want to talk to you, I am so disappointed in you" are examples of parents using love withdrawal or guilt induction to control their children. While such parental tactics may temporarily control behavior, this type of discipline destroys teens' sense of self-worth and their confidence in their own ability to make good decisions. It is one thing to make a mistake—it is an entirely different thing to be "stupid," "lazy," or "no good." Words do indeed have meaning, and teens who experience this type of parental control come to believe their parents when they say that they are worthless. With their feelings of self-worth destroyed, they withdraw within themselves and try to regain their parents' acceptance by becoming overly dependent on them.

We are not saying that parents shouldn't disapprove of their teenagers' violation of family rules, disobeying gospel standards, or not putting reasonable effort in school. What we are saying is that disapproval and appropriate discipline need to be expressed within the context of love and understanding, as expressed by the Lord in the scriptures (see D&C 121:41–45). Speaking in the general priesthood session of the April 1983 general conference, Jeffrey R. Holland, then president of Brigham Young University, told a painful personal experience that powerfully illustrates this concept:

> Early in our married life my young family and I were laboring through graduate school at a university in New England. Pat was the Relief Society president in our ward, and I was serving in our stake presidency. I was going to school full-time and teaching half-time. We had two small children then, with little money and lots of pressures. In fact, our life was about like yours.
>
> One evening I came home from long hours at school, feeling the proverbial weight of the world on my shoulders. Everything seemed to be especially demanding and discouraging and dark. I wondered if the dawn would ever come. Then, as I walked into our small student apartment, there was an unusual silence in the room.
>
> "What's the trouble?" I asked. "Matthew has something he wants to tell you," Pat said. "Matt, what do you have to tell me?" He was quietly playing with his toys in the corner of the room, trying very hard not to hear me. "Matt," I said a little louder, "do you have something to tell me?"
>
> He stopped playing, but for a moment didn't look up. Then these two enormous, tear-filled brown eyes turned toward me, and with the pain only a five-year-old can know, he said, "I didn't mind Mommy tonight, and I spoke back to her." With that he burst into

tears, and his entire little body shook with grief. A childish indiscretion had been noted, a painful confession had been offered, the growth of a five-year-old was continuing, and loving reconciliation could have been wonderfully underway.

Everything might have been just terrific—except for me. If you can imagine such an idiotic thing, I lost my temper. It wasn't that I lost it with Matt—it was with a hundred and one other things on my mind; but he didn't know that, and I wasn't disciplined enough to admit it. He got the whole load of bricks.

I told him how disappointed I was and how much more I thought I could have expected from him. I sounded like the parental pygmy I was. Then I did what I had never done before in his life—I told him that he was to go straight to bed and that I would not be in to say his prayers with him or to tell him a bedtime story. Muffling his sobs, he obediently went to his bedside, where he knelt—alone—to say his prayers. Then he stained his little pillow with tears his father should have been wiping away.

If you think the silence upon my arrival was heavy, you should have felt it now. Pat did not say a word. She didn't have to. I felt terrible!

Later, as we knelt by our own bed, my feeble prayer for blessings upon my family fell back on my ears with a horrible, hollow ring. I wanted to get up off my knees right then and go to Matt and ask his forgiveness, but he was long since peacefully asleep.

My relief was not so soon coming; but finally I fell asleep and began to dream, which I seldom do. I dreamed Matt and I were packing two cars for a move. For some reason his mother and baby sister were not present. As we finished I turned to him and said, "Okay, Matt, you drive one car and I'll drive the other."

This five-year-old very obediently crawled up on the seat and tried to grasp the massive steering wheel. I walked over to the other car and started the motor. As I began to pull away, I looked to see how my son was doing. He was trying—oh, how he was trying. He tried to reach the pedals, but he couldn't. He was also turning knobs and pushing buttons, trying to start the motor. He could scarcely be seen over the dashboard, but there staring out at me again were those same immense, tear-filled, beautiful brown eyes. As I pulled away, he cried out, "Daddy, don't leave me. I don't know how to do it. I am too little." And I drove away.

A short time later, driving down that desert road in my dream, I suddenly realized in one stark, horrifying moment what I had done. I slammed my car to a stop, threw open the door, and started to run as fast as I could. I left car, keys, belongings, and all—and I ran. The pavement was so hot it burned my feet, and tears blinded my straining effort to see this child somewhere on the horizon. I kept running, praying, pleading to be forgiven and to find my boy safe and secure.

As I rounded a curve nearly ready to drop from physical and emotional exhaustion, I saw the unfamiliar car I had left Matt to drive. It was pulled carefully off to the side of the road, and he was laughing and playing nearby. An older man was with him, playing and responding to his games. Matt saw me and cried out something like, "Hi, Dad. We're having fun." Obviously he had already forgiven and forgotten my terrible transgression against him.

But I dreaded the older man's gaze, which followed my every move. I tried to say "Thank you," but his eyes were filled with sorrow and disappointment. I muttered an awkward apology and the stranger said simply, "You should not have left him alone to do this difficult thing. It would not have been asked of you."

With that, the dream ended, and I shot upright in bed. My pillow was now stained, whether with perspiration or tears I do not know. I threw off the covers and ran to the little metal camp cot that was my son's bed. There on my knees and through my tears I cradled him in my arms and spoke to him while he slept. I told him that every dad makes mistakes but that they don't mean to. I told him it wasn't his fault I had had a bad day. I told him that when boys are five or fifteen, dads sometimes forget and think they are fifty. I told him that

I wanted him to be a small boy for a long, long time, because all too soon he would grow up and be a man and wouldn't be playing on the floor with his toys when I came home. I told him that I loved him and his mother and his sister more than anything in the world and that whatever challenges we had in life we would face them together. I told him that never again would I withhold my affection or my forgiveness from him, and never, I prayed, would he withhold them from me. I told him I was honored to be his father and that I would try with all my heart to be worthy of such a great responsibility. (Conference Report, Apr. 1983, pp. 52–53.)

Those who have read this chapter may feel overwhelmed with all the suggestions. Or they may feel that they have done everything wrong. We certainly don't want to discourage or overwhelm, but neither do we want to minimize the sacred yet weighty responsibilities of being a parent. We believe that implementing some of these practical suggestions will actually make parenting easier and certainly more enjoyable.

Within a loving family, where parents express their love for their children in word and deed and where children feel accepted and valued, it is not difficult to establish family rules, guidelines or principles that will govern family members. Although disciplining teenagers is unpleasant, it is vital in helping them develop the self-control necessary for living in society. Discipline coupled with forgiveness is like repentance—it allows parents and teens to put mistakes, problems, and conflicts behind them. Finally, psychological autonomy will nurture the internalization of values, beliefs, and ideas consistent with gospel principles, which in turn will help a teen mature from the insecurity and uncertainty of junior high into competent adults. These parenting practices can help parents assist their children to realize their potential in the pursuit of education, a happy marriage, a successful career, and activity in the gospel kingdom.

142

Our research and experience as youth leaders and parents ourselves confirm that families who in their own way have incorporated these practices are happier. Parents enjoy their teens, and the teens actually like their parents—although they may still be embarrassed to be seen in public with them. In addition, parents watch with pride as their teenage children steadily make the transition into adulthood. Perhaps the greatest fulfillment any parent can feel is to have their adult children as their "best friends."

# 6

# HELP FROM BEYOND
# THE VEIL

## THE POWER OF THE COVENANT

In this day and age the responsibilities of parenthood—of teaching the gospel, training children in vital skills, monitoring activities and friends, protecting from the many evil influences—can seem overwhelming. It is difficult enough just to try to keep track of the fast pace "comings and goings" of teenagers, let alone all the other things that should be done in their behalf. It is easy to become discouraged when it seems that nothing we do seems to be influencing our children or when we compare our families with others and wonder what went wrong. This kind of discouragement is compounded when we read parenting books or hear talks about what we should be doing in our homes, and then we particularly observe where we seem to be falling short. Statements such as "I wish I would have done" or "we need to be doing" or "we shouldn't have allowed" or "things would be better if" sometimes become billy clubs with which to beat ourselves over the head instead of serving as motivational evaluation. All parents experience some degree of regret—wishing they would have done things differently or been smarter or more loving. Learning new skills, learning from our mistakes, repenting, changing—all are part of the process of becoming good parents, part of the schooling of mortality that helps us become celestial parents in eternity. Even when we know this in our heads, however, it doesn't always compute that way in our hearts when we see our children stray from the path of the gospel or become estranged from our family in any way. It is natural to blame ourselves for these perceived failures.

Sometimes the teachings of the prophets regarding the role of the family and the responsibilities of parents can be seen as a two-edged sword—one edge teaching us the doctrine of eternal families and motivating us to be faithful and loving parents. This can be seen in the following statement of President Joseph F. Smith:

There is too little religious devotion, love and fear of God in the home; too much worldliness, selfishness, indifference and lack of reverence in the family or these would never exist so abundantly on the outside. Then the home is what needs reforming. Try today, and tomorrow, to make a change in your home by praying twice a day with your family; call on your children and your wife to pray with you. Ask a blessing upon every meal you eat. Spend ten minutes in reading a chapter from the words of the Lord in the Bible, the Book of Mormon, the Doctrine and Covenants, before you retire or before you go to your daily toil. Feed your spiritual selves at home, as well as in public lives. Let love, and peace, and the Spirit of the Lord, kindness, charity, sacrifice for others abound in your families. Banish harsh words, envyings, hatreds, evil speaking, obscene language and innuendo, blasphemy, and let the Spirit of God take possession of your hearts. Teach your children these things, in spirit and power, sustained and strengthened by personal practice. Let them see that you are earnest, and practice what you preach. Do not let your children out to specialists in these things, but teach them by your own precept and example, by your own fireside. Be a specialist yourself in truth. Let our meetings, schools, and organizations, instead of being our only or leading teachers, be supplements to our teachings and training in the home. Not one child in a hundred would go astray, if the home environment, example and training, were in harmony with the truth in the gospel of Christ, as revealed and taught to the Latter-day Saints. Fathers and mothers, you are largely to blame for the infidelity and indifference of your children. You can remedy the evil by earnest worship, example, training, and discipline in the home. (*Gospel Doctrine* [Salt Lake City: Deseret Book Co., 1939], pp. 301–2.)

The second edge of the sword is seen in the last part of this prophetic statement—the indictment against parents, the prescription for "remedy" and the promise that "not one child in a hundred would go astray" if parents would follow this counsel. We bear testimony of the truthfulness of principles included in President Smith's statement. While the principles remain the same, the conditions in the world that affect families, parents, and children have changed dramatically since President Smith uttered that promise. Perhaps even his promise now has to be modified in light of the prevailing wickedness of the world. Even this thought, however, is a double-edged sword.

The piercing, double edge of President Smith's statement (and other prophetic statements like this) comes when we define it by our own limited definitions and timetables rather than with God's eternal perspective. This other edge then pierces our hearts with guilt and discouragement when things don't go as smoothly in raising our families as we had hoped or expected. This painful piercing is compounded when parents have indeed done all that the prophets have taught, yet their children choose to follow a different path in life. It is one of the difficult ironies of life—parents who conscientiously seek to live and teach the gospel in their home and who seem to do all the right things yet their children go astray; on the other hand we see faithful, spiritually strong, competent and committed children who "turned out right" despite being raised in extremely difficult circumstances or by parents who did all the wrong things.

Unfortunately, there is no magic formula for raising righteous children, no protective coating we can spray on them that will repel all evil in their lives. Unlike baking cookies, there is no recipe card for producing righteous children, which, if we follow directions precisely and include all the best ingredients, such as spirituality, family connectedness, regulation, and psychological autonomy, will automatically produce celestial children. We can only do so much, but there are still many other influences at work—opposition, evil influences, friends, Church programs and teachings, individual agency, and even the spiritual traits and tendencies a child brings from the premortal world.

Despite this, there is comfort to be had. "It is a great challenge to raise a family in the darkening mists of our moral environment," Elder Boyd K. Packer observed.

> We emphasize that the greatest work you will do will be within the walls of your home (see Harold B. Lee, Conference Report, Apr. 1973, p. 130; or *Ensign,* July 1973, p. 98), and that "no other success can compensate for failure in the home" (see David O. McKay, Conference Report, Apr. 1935, p. 116; quoting J. E. McCulloch, *Home: The Savior of Civilization* [Washington, D.C.: The Southern Co-operative League, 1924], p. 42).

> The measure of our success as parents, however, will not rest solely on how our children turn out. That judgment would be just only if we could raise our families in a perfectly moral environment, and that now is not possible.

> It is not uncommon for responsible parents to lose one of their children, for a time, to influences over which they have no control. They agonize over rebellious sons or daughters. They are puzzled

over why they are so helpless when they have tried so hard to do what they should.

It is my conviction that those wicked influences one day will be overruled. (Conference Report, Apr. 1992, pp. 94–95.)

The great news of the gospel is that, as Elder Packer testified, "those wicked influences one day will be overruled." That message should be comforting to parents as they raise their children and as they agonize over the apparent loss of a prodigal. When parents feel totally surrounded by evil and it seems that nothing they do as parents can save their children from the ways of the world, they feel to ask the question, *"How and when will these wicked influences be overruled?"*

From the inspiring story of an Old Testament prophet, we can begin to see an answer, one that can comfort parents and also guide them in their responsibilities. It is the account of the divine protection afforded the prophet Elisha when he was surrounded by the Syrian army.

The kingdom of Israel had been invaded from the north by the Syrians. Under the inspiration of God, Elisha had warned the Israelite king of the invasion and counseled him on how to wage war against the Syrians. When the Syrian king was apprised of the fact that the Israelite prophet was counseling the king of Israel regarding the positions and strategies of the Syrian army, he sent horses, chariots, and numerous soldiers to surround the city and capture Elisha. "And when the servant of the man of God was risen early, and gone forth, behold, an host compassed the city both with horses and chariots. And his servant said unto him, Alas, my master! how shall we do?" (2 Kings 6:15.) In modern vernacular, the servant is really asking the prophet, "How are we going to get out of this mess? We are totally surrounded!"

Elisha's response may have caused the young servant boy to think the prophet was crazy or talking in his sleep. "Fear not," Elisha declared to the young man, "for they that be with us are more than they that be with them" (2 Kings 6:16). How could that be? As the servant boy looked around them, all he could see was hundreds of Syrian soldiers armed with swords and spears, riding on their horses and in their chariots. How could anybody in his right mind make such a statement, "They that be with us are more than they that be with them"? The situation likely appeared completely hopeless to this young man as he surveyed the odds—one young boy and an aged man against an entire army! It didn't look good.

Elisha must have seen the fear and confusion in the boy's eyes. "And Elisha prayed, and said, Lord, I pray thee, open his eyes, that he may see. And the Lord opened the eyes of the young man; and he saw: and, behold, the mountain was full of horses and chariots of fire round about Elisha." (2 Kings 6:17.)

If our spiritual eyes could be opened like the eyes of the servant of Elisha, we too would discover that we are not left alone nor forsaken in our battles against evil in the world. There are more powers of good and righteousness within the gospel of Jesus Christ than the powers of wickedness in the world. Perhaps the Lord's promise that he will "cause the heavens to shake for [our] good" (D&C 21:6) is more literal than we often suspect and may have as much application to families as individuals. Even though we as parents may feel surrounded and badly outnumbered by the enemy as we seek to raise our children, the Lord has blessed us with great resources to strengthen and protect our families. He has even promised greater blessings to the faithful that have a profound impact on families. These promised blessings provide the means whereby the evil influences that sorely afflict families today will one day be overruled.

# In the Presence of Angels

In addition to the divine assistance afforded parents in the form of inspired counsel from prophets and apostles, the programs and activities of the Church organization, and the guidance of the Holy Ghost, parents are also aided—sometimes knowingly, but often unknowingly—from beyond the veil. One of the most familiar examples of this is found in the Book of Mormon. Alma the elder surely must have agonized not only over the apostasy of his son Alma the younger but also over the detrimental impact his son's behavior was having on others. We can only imagine the anguish felt by both Alma and his wife over this situation. We can almost see and hear their heartfelt pleadings with the Lord. These prayers did not go unanswered. These parents were not left alone in their earnest efforts to reclaim a son who had strayed so far from the path of truth.

And now it came to pass that while [Alma the younger] was going about to destroy the church of God, for he did go secretly with the sons of Mosiah seeking to destroy the church, and to lead astray the people of the Lord, contrary to the commandments of God, or even the king—

And as I said unto you, as they were going about rebelling against God, behold the angel of the Lord appeared unto them; and he descended as it were in a cloud; and he spake as it were with a voice of thunder, which caused the earth to shake upon which they stood;

And so great was their astonishment, that they fell to the earth, and understood not the words which he spake unto them.

Nevertheless he cried again, saying: Alma, arise and stand forth, for why persecutest thou the church of God? for the Lord hath said: This is my church, and I will establish it; and nothing can overthrow it, save the transgression of my people.

And again the angel said: Behold, the Lord hath heard the prayers of his people, and also the prayers of his servant, Alma, who is thy father; for he has prayed with much faith concerning thee that thou mightest be brought to the knowledge of the truth; therefore, for this purpose have I come to convince thee of the power and authority of God, that the prayers of his servants might be answered according to their faith. (Mosiah 27:10–14.)

The rebellious son's life was turned around through a marvelous manifestation from an angel of God—on account of the faith and prayers of his parents! Some parents may read this and ask, "Why hasn't the Lord sent an angel to reclaim my wayward son or daughter? Haven't I prayed and exercised as much faith as Alma?" This scriptural example should not cause us to feel badly or less worthy of a miracle than Alma but rather should give us hope. This hope then, in turn, can motivate us to never cease praying for all the divine help we can get as parents—help even from beyond the veil. It may be that while we ponder the visit of an angel to the young Alma and ask "why not for my child?" we are at that moment receiving unseen support and help. It may not be as visible or dramatic as Alma's experience, but it can be nonetheless as miraculous and life changing.

"I will go before your face," the Lord has promised faithful parents and individuals. "I will be on your right hand and on your left, and my Spirit shall be in your hearts, and mine angels round about you, to bear you up" (D&C 84:88). Families are not forsaken of the Lord in these troubled times. Parents are not left alone in their weighty and eternally significant responsibilities. Probably more than we realize, we are receiving help in guiding, directing, and protecting our families from beyond the veil. "God loves us. He's watching us, he wants us to succeed," President Ezra Taft Benson testified, "and we'll know someday that he has not left one thing undone for the eternal welfare of each of us. If we only knew it, there are heavenly hosts pulling for us—friends in heaven that we can't remember now, who yearn for our victory." ("Insights: We Seek That Which Is Praiseworthy," *Ensign*, July 1975, p. 63.)

There is at least as much, if not more, love and concern for family members on the other side of the veil in the hearts of departed loved ones as there is for earthly parents. The faith and prayers and diligent efforts of parents for their children can only be aided and strengthened with the combined diligence, compassion, concern, and sometimes even intervention of loved ones beyond the veil. This is illustrated with the following experience from the life of Elder Bruce R. McConkie. When his beloved father, Oscar McConkie Sr., approached the time of death, he gathered his family around him and declared, "I am going to die. When I die I shall not cease to love you. I shall not cease to pray for you. I shall not cease to labor in your behalf." (As quoted by Robert L. Millet, *When a Child Wanders* [Salt Lake City: Deseret Book Co., 1996], p. 133.) We, as parents and grandparents, would all feel this way. What a wonderful promise of help and hope for families is found in this doctrine, as taught by President Joseph F. Smith!

Sometimes the Lord expands our vision from this point of view and this side of the veil, so that we feel and seem to realize that we can look beyond the thin veil which separates us from that other sphere. If we can see, by the enlightening influence of the Spirit of God and through the words that have been spoken by the holy prophets of God, beyond the veil that separates us from the spirit world, surely those who have passed beyond, can see more clearly through the veil back here to us than it is possible for us to see to them from our sphere of action. I believe we move and have our being in the presence of heavenly messengers and of heavenly beings. We are not separate from them. We begin to realize, more and more fully, as we become acquainted with the principles of the gospel, as they have been revealed anew in this dispensation, that we are closely related to our kindred, to our ancestors, to our friends and associates and co-laborers who have preceded us into the spirit world. We can not forget them; we do not cease to love them; we always hold them in our hearts, in memory, and thus we are associated and united to them by ties that we cannot break, that we cannot dissolve or free ourselves from. . . . And therefore, I claim that we live in their presence, they see us, they are solicitous for our welfare, they love us now more than ever. For now they see the dangers that beset us; they can comprehend, better than ever before, the weaknesses that are liable to mislead us into dark and forbidden paths. They see the temptations and the evils that beset us in life, and the proneness of mortal beings to yield to temptation and to wrong doing; hence their solicitude for us and their love for us and their desire for our well being must be greater than that which we feel for ourselves. . . .

. . . When messengers are sent to minister to the inhabitants of this earth, they are not strangers, but from the ranks of our kindred, friends, and fellow-beings and fellow-servants. . . . In like manner, our fathers and mothers, brothers, sisters, and friends who have passed away from this earth, having been faithful, and worthy to enjoy these rights and privileges, may have a mission given them to visit their relatives and friends upon the earth again, bringing from the divine Presence messages of love, of warning, or reproof and instruction, to those whom they had learned to love in the flesh. (*Gospel Doctrine* [Salt Lake City: Deseret Book Co., 1939], pp. 430–31, 435–36.)

# The Redemptive Power of Covenants

Even with the promise of divine assistance from beyond the veil, some parents may still feel that there is no hope for reclaiming a lost daughter or son. It may appear that all parental efforts have failed, that all familial support has eroded, that no divine ear is listening to their pleadings, and hope for an Alma-like miracle has faded. But there is a power afforded to families greater than all earthly efforts of home and Church combined. This power is even greater than the ministrations of angels. It is the redemptive power of the covenant. It is of this power that Elder Packer was speaking when he expressed his conviction that "those wicked influences one day will be over-ruled." He explained:

> We cannot overemphasize the value of temple marriage, the binding ties of the sealing ordinance, and the standards of worthiness required of them. When parents keep the covenants they have made at the altar of the temple, their children will be forever bound to them. (In Conference Report, Apr. 1992, p. 95.)

This is certainly not to say that we, as parents, can neglect, shirk, or even defy the spiritual obligations of parenthood and still have all the blessings of eternal families. It does say, however, as Nephi declared, "that it is by grace that we are saved, after all we can do" (2 Nephi 25:23). We most often think of this passage to apply to individual salvation, but it also applies to the redemption of the family through the covenant of celestial marriage. The "all we can do" as parents is to teach, love, nurture, build testimony, provide spiritual experiences, discipline, monitor, and provide more love and affection. But sometimes even this, in this wicked world, is not enough to keep a child on the gospel path and near our hearts. For this reason the grace of God that can make up the difference is the binding power of the covenant that can ultimately reach a child when all other efforts fail and bring them back to the fold and weld their hearts to ours.

While we do not fully understand how all this operates and will eventually unfold, we are assured of the reality of this hope-anchoring promise. Prophets and apostles have long taught this doctrine. President Brigham Young declared:

> Let the father and mother, who are members of this Church and kingdom, take a righteous course, and strive with all their might never to do wrong, but to do good all their lives, if they have one child or one hundred children, they conduct themselves toward them as they should, bring them to their Lord by their faith and prayers, I care not where those children go, they are bound up to their parents by an everlasting tie, and no power on earth or hell can separate them from their parents in eternity; they will return again to the fountain from whence they sprang. (*Journal of Discourses* 11:215.)

Elder Orson F. Whitney of the Council of the Twelve Apostles similarly declared in general conference of April 1929:

> You parents of the wilful and the wayward! Don't give them up. Don't cast them off. They are not utterly lost. The Shepherd will find his sheep. They were his before they were yours—long before he entrusted them to your care; and you cannot begin to love them as he loves them. They have strayed in ignorance from the Path of Right, and God is merciful to ignorance. Only the fulness of knowledge brings the fulness of accountability. Our Heavenly Father is far more merciful, infinitely more charitable, than even the best of his servants, and the Everlasting Gospel is mightier in power to save than our narrow finite minds can comprehend.
>
> The Prophet Joseph declared—and he never taught a more comforting doctrine—that the eternal sealings of faithful parents and divine promises made to them for valiant service in the Cause of Truth, would save not only themselves, but likewise their poster-

ity. Though some of the sheep may wander, the eye of the Shepherd is upon them, and sooner or later they will feel the tentacles of Divine Providence reaching out after them and drawing them back to the fold. Either in this life or in the life to come, they will return. They will have to pay their debt to justice; they will suffer for their sins; and may tread a thorny path; but if it leads them at last, like the penitent Prodigal, to a loving and forgiving father's heart and home, the painful experience will not have been in vain. Pray for your careless and disobedient children; hold on to them with your faith. Hope on, trust on, till you see the salvation of God. (In Conference Report, Apr. 1929, p. 110.)

President Lorenzo Snow prophetically promised:

God fulfills his promises to us, and our prospects are grand and glorious. Yes, in the next life we will have our wives, and our sons and daughters. If we do not get them all at once, we will have them some time, for every knee shall bow and every tongue shall confess that Jesus is the Christ. You that are mourning about your children straying away will have your sons and daughters. If you succeed in passing through these trials and afflictions and receive a resurrection, you will, by the power of the Priesthood, work and labor, as the Son has, until you get all your sons and daughters in the path of exaltation and glory. This is just as sure as that the sun rose this morning over yonder mountains. There, mourn not because all your sons and daughters do not follow in the path that you have marked out for them, or give heed to your counsels. Inasmuch as we succeed in securing eternal glory, and stand as saviors, and as kings and priests to our God, we will save our posterity. . . .

God will have His own way and His own time, and He will accomplish His purposes in the salvation of His sons and daughters. . . . God bless you, brethren and sisters. Do not be discouraged is the word I wish to pass to you, but remember that righteousness and joy in the Holy Ghost is what you and I have the privilege of possessing at all times. (*Collected Discourses* 3:364–65.)

What glorious promises! What comforting and strengthening counsel to parents! If we are true and faithful to our own covenants and do "all we can do" in loving and leading our families, we are assured of help beyond our own efforts—angels, seen and unseen, will provide protection and direction in times of need. Most significant of all, is the claim upon the redemptive power of the temple covenants we have to save not only ourselves but also our children. When we really understand this doctrine and believe these promises, we can face with faith the challenge of rearing righteous children in this wicked world. This hope in Christ and his sure promises can guide us in our relationships with our families.

Understanding the power of the covenant will affect how we view our children, how we treat them, and how we seek to raise them up unto the Lord. We will never give up hope for we will understand that "after all we can do" for our families, we can look beyond the veil for the saving power that we cannot provide ourselves. There is no greater help for families than that! As President Gordon B. Hinckley has declared: "Now I know that once in a while, notwithstanding all the things you try to do, there is a rebellious child. But keep at it. Do not ever give up. You have never lost as long as you try. Keep at it." ("Inspirational Thoughts," *Ensign*, August 1997, p. 4.)

"Train up a child in the way he should go:
and when he is old, he will not depart from it."
—Proverbs 22:6

# Index

— A —

Acceptance in Church, 20
Activities, importance of participation in, 55–56
Affection, 101; of fathers, 103
Agency, 148
Alma, 88, 151–52
Angels, help parents, 158
Asch, Solomon, 48

— B —

Bad situations, avoiding, 61–62
Ballard, M. Russell, on role of home, 21–22, 77
Barber, Brian, 8
Barr, William, 3
Benson, Ezra Taft: on iniquity in last days, 2–3, 25; on immorality, 31, 36; promise to youth, 87–88; on seminary attendance, 91; on father's duties, 103; on God helping parents, 152
Blakeslee, Sandra, 14

Blessings, father's, 113–14
Brothers, Joyce, 39
Brown, Victor L., on war between good and evil, 2

— C —

Chastity, talking about, 39
Cheating, 29–30
Chores, 129
Christensen, Joe J., on creating spiritual environment, 77
Church: helps parents, 151; influence of, 44
Clarke, J. Reuben, Jr., on mercy, 112
Communication, 137
Compartmentalization, danger of, 86
Compromise, 60
Connectedness, 15, 100–103; to fathers, 102–3; parents can foster, 104
Conscience, 75
Contention, 114–16

Cornwall, Marie, 8
Councils, family, 119
Covenants, power of, 154–58
Crime, among teenagers, 5
Criticism, 109–11

— D —

Dating: before sixteen, 35; non-
   members, 33, 35, 58
Delinquency: deterring, 74; and em-
   ployment, 91–93; LDS compared
   to others, 26; and peer pressure,
   41, 53, 65; spirituality factor in
   avoiding, 72
Delinquent activities, 29
Delinquent behaviors, avoiding, 56
Discipline, 117, 123–29, 142
Discouragement, 146–47, 157–58
Divorce, 14–15; rates, 3
Drinking, 29–30, 49
Drug use, 28

— E —

Elisha, 149–50
Empathy, 112
Expression, allowing freedom of,
   133–35
Eyring, Henry B., on Holy Ghost a
   gift for families, 79

— F —

Faith, 10
Family: activities, 64; basic unit of
   society, 22, 77; conflict, 14–15;
connectedness, 101–3; councils,
   119; destruction of, 3–4; effect on
   delinquency, 43; emotional
   support of, 13; friendships of,
   54–55; influence of, 44; interaction, 106–7; meals, 104–5; not
   forsaken, 152; prayer, 80–83, 99;
   religious practices, 73; scripture
   study, 80–83; singleparent, 43;
   time together, 105; traditions,
   112–13; two-parent, 43
Family bonds, discourage lying, 122
Family home evening, 80–83,
   99–100; blessings of, 83
Family prayer, 80–83
Family rules, 117–18; monitoring
   of, 121–22; provide structure,
   119; youth should give input to,
   120–21
Fathers: affection of, 103; blessings,
   113–14; connection to, 102–3;
   express love, 116; monitoring of
   youth, 117–18; role of, 103; to
   teach gospel, 103
Faust, James E., on internalizing
   values, 74–75
Fighting, 29
Forgiveness, 111–12
Fornication, 35
Fox, James Alan, 5
Friends, 8–9, 45; from church, 57;
   influence of, 47; selecting good,
   54

— G —

Gospel: has power to save, 156;

power to help youth, 76; sharing feelings about, 85–86
Gospel principles: application of, 83–84; must be internalized, 77
Grace, of God, 155
Grounding, 125
Guilt, 129, 131, 138

— H —

Helaman, 95
Hinckley, Gordon B.: on not giving up on children, 158; on teaching values, 97–98
Hirschi, Travis, 11
Holland, Jeffrey R., incident with son, 139–42
Holy Ghost, 79–80, 158; helps parents, 151
Home: foundation for strength, 97; needs reforming, 146; place to feed spiritual selves, 146; place to hang out, 59
Homicide, teen, 4
Hope: in Christ, 158; for parents, 156–58; for wayward children, 152
Hunter, Howard W., on expressing love, 116
Hymns, 85
Hypocrisy, 79

— I —

Identity, sense of, 47
Illegitimacy, 3
Immorality, 31–32

— J —

Jesus Christ, 67, 150, 152; Second Coming of, 2

— K —

Kimball, Heber C., on gaining own light, 93
Kimball, Spencer W.: on dating, 35; on motivating youth, 74; on seminary attendance, 91

— L —

LDS families, similarity of, 98–99
LDS youth: in mission field, 49–53, 71; pressures facing, 31; study of, 7–8; in Utah County, 51, 70–71
Lee, Harold B., on home, 148
Leniency, 16
Light, must gain own, 93
Lord. See Jesus Christ
Love: expression of, 107–9; following discipline, 129; unconditional, 111; withdrawal of, 131, 138
Lying, 30

— M —

Marriage, temple, 155
Maternal employment, 15, 43
McConkie, Bruce R., experience with father, 153
McConkie, Oscar Sr., 153
McCulloch, J. E., 148
McKay, David O., on home, 148

Meals, with family, 104–5
Meetings, attendance at, 70
Monitoring, family rules, 121–22
*Monitoring the Future,* 26–28
Mothers: employment of, 15, 43; express love, 116; monitoring of youth, 117–18
Movies, 32

— N —

Necking, 35
Neighborhood, influence of, 54
Nephi, 84, 88, 94, 155
Nerds, 9
*Newsweek* (magazine), 104

— O —

Ophelia, 47

— P —

Packer, Boyd K.: on chastity, 32; on raising children, 148; on temple marriage, 155
Parental disapproval, 62
Parenthood, challenge of, 7
Parents: advice to, 37–38; allow free expression, 136; can foster connectedness, 104; can help youth internalize gospel, 77; can influence friend choices, 54–59; challenges facing, 65; confiding in, 62–63; contention between, 114–16; create spiritual environment, 77; discouragement of, 145–46; encouragement for, 149; example of, 78–80; express love, 116; how to help youth, 47, 78–95; hypocrisy in, 79; love each other, 114; make friends welcome, 59; monitoring peers, 63–64; to monitor youth, 117; need to be strict, 120; not forsaken, 152; not to impose self on youth, 137–38; promise to, 157; responsible to love, 97; role in shaping youth, 14; should host activities, 57; should listen, 136; should praise youth, 109; should teach chastity, 36; success of, 148; support youth in activities, 105; to teach, 146–47; to teach gospel, 83–84; teach responsibility, 130; unity of, 128; ways to spend time with youth, 106
Paul the Apostle, 1, 67, 87
Peer example, 42
Peer pressure, 6, 40–41; factor in youth behavior, 8, 45–49; as negative force, 51–53; overcoming, 75–76; resisting, 60–65; study demonstrating, 48–49; two types of, 9–10
Peers, influence of, 44
Perry, L. Tom, on teaching responsibility, 130
Peterson, H. Burke, on loving children, 110
Petting, 29, 31, 35
Pipher, Mary, 46–47
Pornography, 31
Pray, for children, 157

Prayer: family, 99; importance of, 87–89
Pregnancy, 4
Premarital sex, 31–32, 51
Private religious behavior, 19, 70–71
Prophets, help parents, 151
Psychological autonomy, 16, 43, 101, 131–43
Public religious behavior, 19, 70
Punishment, types of, 125–27

— Q —

Questions, answering hard, 90

— R —

Regulation, 15, 100–101; of youth, 117–31
Relationships, with God, 68
Religion: and delinquency, 11; effect on behavior, 68
Religiosity, 70–71, 78; among youth, 11–12; five dimensions of, 13, 72; influences behavior, 42–43, 67; relationship to delinquency, 72–77
Religious behavior, 19
Religious ecology, 17; theory, 12, 40
Religious values, 11
Responsibility, teaching of, 130

— S —

Satan, 2, 25–27; assault on youth, 4

Saturday's Warriors, 25–26
Saturday warriors, 2
Scripture study, 80–83; importance of, 87–89
Self-control, teaching youth, 118
Self-destructive behavior, 5
Seminary: influence of, 90–91; youth should attend, 90–91
Service, 85
Sex, casual, 38; oral, 38; premarital, 31–32
Sexual intercourse, 29, 31, 33
Shoplifting, 29
Sibling conflicts, 124
Sin, sense of, confused, 48
Singing, 85
Situations, avoiding bad, 61–62
Smith, Joseph: on faith of parents, 156; on love, 129; on sexual sin, 31
Smith, Joseph F.: on divine help, 153; on loving children, 116; on reforming the home, 146–47
Smoking, 29–30
Snow, Lorenzo, a prophetic promise, 157
Social acceptance, 73
Social skills, importance of, 55
Spirit, helping youth feel, 84–85
Spiritual experiences, 20, 84–85; gaining, 77–78
Spiritual intimacy, 114
Spirituality: factor in avoiding delinquency, 72; internal vs. external, 76; personal, 74, 84–85, 95
Spouse, love and honor, 114

Standards: declare to friends, 61; double, 79

Stark, Rodney, 11

Structure equation analysis, 21

Study of LDS youth, 7–8

Substance abuse, 4, 28–29, 51

Suicide, 4

Sunday, working on, 91–94

— T —

Talking: about the gospel, 85–86; importance of, 62–63, 86

Teen pregnancy, 4

Television, 32

Temptation, resisting, 67, 88–89

Testimony, 80, 85; gaining, 77–78; importance of, 94

Thomas, Darwin, 8

Traditions, family, 112–13

Trespassing, 29

— V —

Values: deterioration of, 32; take a stand on, 60–61

Vandalizing, 29

— W —

Wallerstein, Judith S., 14

War, between good and evil, 2

Whitney, Orson F., on not giving up, 156

Word of Wisdom, 30

— Y —

Young, Brigham, on faith of parents, 156

Youth: encourage to express themselves, 136; encourage to gain testimony, 93–95; need expressions of love, 108–9; need praise, 109; polarization of, 6; temptations of, 5

— Z —

Zion, 41